THE RIGHT WAY TO ROCK

BOOKS BY NAT AMOORE

Secrets of a Schoolyard Millionaire
The Power of Positive Pranking
The Right Way to Rock

We Run Tomorrow

THE RIGHT WAY TO ROCK

NAT AMOORE

PUFFIN BOOKS

For JC. You rock!

PUFFIN BOOKS

UK | USA | Canada | Ireland | Australia
India | New Zealand | South Africa | China

Penguin Random House Australia

Penguin Random House Australia is part of the Penguin Random House group of companies whose addresses can be found at global.penguinrandomhouse.com.

First published by Puffin Books, an imprint of Penguin Random House Australia Pty Ltd, in 2021

Cover illustrations by James Lancett
Internal images: lightning and swirl © James Lancett, musical notes © mhatzapa/Shutterstock.com
Cover design by Tony Palmer © Penguin Random House Australia Pty Ltd
Text design based on series design by Tony Palmer © Penguin Random House Australia Pty Ltd

NATIONAL LIBRARY OF AUSTRALIA

A catalogue record for this book is available from the National Library of Australia

Printed and bound in Australia by Griffin Press, an accredited ISO AS/NZS 14001 Environmental Management Systems printer

ISBN 978 1 76 089770 3

Penguin Random House Australia uses papers that are natural and recyclable products, made from wood grown in sustainable forests. The logging and manufacture processes are expected to conform to the environmental regulations of the country of origin.

penguin.com.au

SCENES

ACT ONE
Scene One

Mac Cooper's Bedroom

The sounds of Watterson create a rhythm. The honk of a car horn, the ding of a bicycle bell, the thud of roadworks. The beat builds up, providing a soundtrack to MAC COOPER's awakening. He leaps out of bed, throwing the curtains wide open as sunlight streams onto his face like a spotlight and a bluebird lands on the windowsill. Mac sings to the street . . .

'Good Morning Watterson'

(to the tune of 'Good Morning Baltimore'
from *Hairspray*)

Good morning Watterson!
Every day promises more fun
Every night is a wistful dream
Every kid has a brilliant scheme.

Good morning Watterson!
And some day when all's said and done
No matter how far I might roam
Watterson is home.

'Mac Fleetwood Cooper! You'd better be in the shower already!'

I press stop on Mum's old iPhone, cutting off my musical alarm and abruptly ending my show-stopping performance. Mum bursts through my bedroom door, but she's definitely not here to give me a standing ovation.

'Shower. Now!' she yells as she fights with the inside-out t-shirt in her grip.

'Muuuum!' I yell. 'What happened to knocking?'

She mumbles at me through the fabric as she yanks the tee down over her messy hair. 'I'll start knocking when you start being able to get yourself into the shower before every other kid is already in first class.'

She tugs on the bottom of her faded Fleetwood Mac t-shirt and tries to pat down her hair. A hairbrush might have more effect, but she's got that 'don't push me' look in her eye so I don't suggest it.

'Well?' she says, glaring at me like one wrong move will have me babysitting Stevie for eternity. I look over what I call her 'uniform'. Mum's wardrobe looks like Bart Simpson's, but instead of a whole heap of blue shorts and red shirts, it's faded rock-band tees and ripped jeans (which she actually paid for – the rips, I mean).

Mum grabs hold of the sides of her hair. 'I swear to Gwen Stefani, if you are not in the shower by the count of three, Mac, I'll . . .'

I don't wait to hear the end of it. I duck past her and bolt for the bathroom, moulting clothes onto the floor as I go. Stevie's sitting in the middle of the hall playing Lego in his undies. I hurdle him, yelling, 'Stevie, DUCK!'

'Duck, duck, goose!' he sings, not ducking even the slightest bit, but I clear his head with ease.

Within 45 seconds, I'm in the shower and have avoided the wrath of Morning Mum.

Morning Mum is not my real mum. She's some kind of monster that comes from finishing work at 2 am and having to get two boys ready and out the door before 8:30 am. My real mum's pretty cool and chill, and even a bit patient. Morning Mum is *none* of those things. You don't mess with Morning Mum.

I tilt my head back and the warm water drums out a beat on my forehead. I can't stay in here for too long, but if I skip washing my hair, I'll have time for one song. I grab Mum's back scrubber and flip through the songbook in my head. I land on 'Consider Yourself' from *Oliver!* and flick on my imaginary top hat. I raise the scrubbing brush to my lips and belt out the words in my best cockney accent, my singing muffled by the bathroom fan and the pelting water.

I barely get to the first chorus before Morning Mum is screeching at me again, so I put away my microphone-brush and finish actually washing myself.

'I shouldn't have to be on your back in the mornings anymore, Mac,' Mum says as I make my way into the kitchen. 'You're going to be in high school next year. High school! The least you can do is get yourself ready on time.'

'Time, Mr Wolf. What's the time?' Stevie yells out. Mum dumps a bowl of soggy cornflakes in front of him.

I fill my own bowl and Mum rages a breakfast war with Stevie, who is totally capable of feeding himself but totally bored by it at the same time. High school next year. A feeling of dread creeps over me. I want to think it's going to be just like *High School Musical*. All of us dressed in crisp red and white uniforms, singing about how 'We're All In This Together', but my guess is that the reality is far less boppy. The local high school colours are brown and yellow too, which is just gross.

'Have you got band practice today?' Mum asks. She watches Stevie through narrowed eyes as he attempts to get the cornflake-filled spoon into his mouth using his left hand. Stevie is right-handed, but he likes a challenge.

He fails miserably, sending soggy flakes splattering over Mum's face. 'Stevie Nick Cooper!' she yells. Mum loves using our full names when we're in trouble. I was named after the band Fleetwood Mac and Stevie was named after their lead singer, Stevie Nicks. She thinks that's pretty clever. I just find it kind of embarrassing. And a bit sad that we didn't even get our own names – we're just borrowing someone else's. If you haven't guessed by the t-shirts and our names, Mum is a big fan of rock bands. Like a BIG fan. With Fleetwood Mac being the number one supreme rock band of all time – Mum's words, not mine.

'Yeah, I've got practice after school.' I pour milk on my cereal and wait for it to go soggy.

'School bell. Ring ring!' shouts Stevie, dropping another left-handed spoonful of flakes and milk. Half of it splashes up into Mum's hair and the other half drips onto his bare legs. I notice Mum isn't giving *him* a 'you're going to be in primary school next year, the least you can do is wear pants' lecture.

Mum throws a cloth at Stevie. 'I give up!' she says, picking soggy flakes out of her hair. She points at me, a little bit of cornflake mush hanging from the end of her finger. 'Tell your brother to eat like a normal kid.'

'Here,' I say, moving to sit next to Stevie. 'Let's try with our right hand BUT we have to eat one spoon every count of eight.' I take my phone out of my pocket and find Stevie's playlist. Tones and I bops through the speaker.

'"Dance Monkey!"' Stevie coos.

'That's right,' I say. 'But only if you eat your breakfast. With your *right* hand!'

Stevie slides back in his chair, picks up his spoon and eats in unison with me. One spoonful on every count of eight as Tones asks us to dance for her.

'I don't know why he likes this song so much,' says Mum as she throws together our lunches. 'I've tried all the *really* good bands, but they just don't have the same effect.'

Stevie's already halfway through his cereal as he bops away and chews in time to the beat. I point that out to Mum. 'I don't know why you fight it.

If he likes it, and it makes him stop throwing food at you, then why not let him listen?'

She shrugs. 'I know, but I just want him to appreciate REAL music.'

Mum has a very narrow view of 'real' music. It's like a pyramid of rock. Fleetwood Mac are perched right at the top, untouched by any other band in the history of music, and then all her 90s favourites sit just below – No Doubt, Alanis Morrisette, The Cranberries. Then everything that isn't rock is unacceptable. So, if she doesn't approve of Stevie's love of indie pop, it should be easy to see why I keep my Broadway performances strictly for the shower.

'He's five, Mum! Last week his favourite song was Baby Shark. I wouldn't be too worried about his musical appreciation just yet.' I go back to stabbing at my cereal.

Bread slips across the kitchen bench as Mum slaps on way too much peanut butter. 'It's never too early to make sure he's on the right path. He's got great rhythm, you know? I think he's gonna be a drummer. I've already asked about lessons.'

This doesn't surprise me at all. She had me in guitar lessons at four, so she probably considers Stevie a slow starter.

Mum whacks the bread together and wraps the pretty rough-looking sandwiches in cling wrap. 'I start at five tonight, so Mrs Moshie will be here from four.' She throws the mangled sandwiches in our lunch boxes, topping the whole thing off with a piece of fruit, and slides them to the end of the counter. 'Do you want me to drop Stevie off or can you take him?'

'I'll take him.' I clear Stevie's empty bowl as he slips down off his chair. I stop him before he skips away. '*If* you can be ready before the end of the next song.'

'What is it?' Stevie says, holding his breath and waiting.

The next track on his playlist starts – 'The Kids Are Coming' by Tones and I.

I grin at him. 'Your favourite!'

Stevie puts his hands on my cheeks and squishes my face together. 'Your favourite brother is me!' he yells, and bolts into his bedroom to get dressed.

Lately he's got this habit of taking the last word you say and turning it into another sentence. It's really annoying and ridiculously cute. But that sums Stevie up perfectly.

'I'll take that as a yes,' I shout after him.

I finish packing my school bag before Stevie comes back, then take his hand. Mum covers both our faces in kisses and herds us out towards the door. 'Make sure you're straight home after practice, Mac. I'll pick Stevie up.'

I pause in the hall. 'Actually, Mum, I'm supposed to make this solar system thing for school and I haven't even started. Maybe I could ask Ms Fox if it's okay to skip band practice and get it done?'

Mum looks at me like I just asked if I could sell Stevie to the second-hand store. 'Miss band practice?' She pulls Stevie's bag up on his shoulders. 'No way. Don't worry, I'll sort the solar system thing for you.'

'Mum! It's MY homework. You can't do it for me.'

She rolls her eyes. 'Band practice will do more for your rock career than painting a few styrofoam balls ever will.'

'Mum!'

'Okay, fine. Go to practice and then I'll *help* you with the project. If we don't get it done on time, I'll talk to Mr Deery. He'll understand that you can't let Ms Fox or the rest of the band down. You have commitments.'

I throw my own bag over my shoulder. 'I think Mr D probably considers schoolwork a commitment too, Mum.'

'Ha ha,' Mum says sarcastically as she pushes us out the door. 'Put it this way: do you want to be an astronaut?'

'No.'

'Exactly! You want to be a rock star and rock stars have to prioritise their music. Now get to school and be good.'

'Good luck with that!' Stevie yells as he waves goodbye.

Mum shuts the door behind us.

I close my eyes for a second and practise the words in my head for the gazillionth time. *I don't want to be a rock star either, Mum.* I wonder what that would sound like out loud.

'C'mon on,' Stevie says, yanking on my hand. 'I wanna get to school.'

'Said no kid ever,' I mumble under my breath, and let myself be dragged off down our street.

'You want to go by Howard Street or through Brennan Park?' I ask.

'Park the car. Brennan Park.'

'Brennan Park it is.'

'Is Wizz Fizz.' He grins at me as we cross the road and walk onto the grass.

Stevie's little legs work double-time to keep up with me as we rush past the Lego house and towards Town Hall. I peek through one of the Lego windows, but can't see any sign of Kathy or her pet ferret, Mr Piddles. They must have had an early start today.

Stevie tugs on my hand. 'Can you do the tango, Mac?'

'Again?'

'Pleeeeeeeeease cheese!' Stevie begs.

What he wants is the song 'Cell Block Tango' from the musical *Chicago*. I do my own version with any words or sounds that Stevie picks.

'All right, so what do you want?'

He looks around and points at some dog poo on the ground. 'Poop!'

Gotta laugh at that. 'Okay. And?'

He spots the ducks at the nearby pond. 'Quack! And fish.'

'Good choices. Now we need a two-beat word and some longer ones.'

'Bon bon. Macaroni. And . . .'

A woman rushes by us, putting on lipstick while looking in the camera of her mobile phone. 'Lipstick!' sings Stevie.

I laugh. 'Those words work perfectly, Stevie. You're getting good at this. I'll start, then you join in and help me, all right?'

'All right, all left.'

I tap my hand against my leg to give us a beat.

```
Poop. Quack. Fish. Bon bon. Macaroni.
              Lipstick.
```

Stevie joins in.

Poop. Quack. Fish. Bon bon. Macaroni.
Lipstick.

Stevie continues as I make up the verse.

They should be runnin'
They should be runnin'
They really should pick up the pace.
But they are walkin'
And they are talkin'
I bet I'll beat you in a race!

I let go of Stevie's hand and run across the park.

'No fair. Head start!' he screams, running after me.

He's right. It's not fair. But it's the ONLY way I'm going to get to school on time and I really don't need to be late again.

'Faster!' I yell over my shoulder. 'Last one there gives Mrs Moshie a foot massage.'

It's cruel, I know, but sometimes a big brother's gotta do what a big brother's gotta do. And *this* big brother's gotta be on time for school.

ACT ONE

Scene Two

Mr Deery's Classroom

Kids sit at their desks, chatting among themselves. MR DEERY, the teacher, arranges his papers as he waits for the school day to begin. Mac rushes in, sliding into his chair just before the bell rings. Written on the whiteboard is one of Mr Deery's corny welcome messages – 'Another day of glorious school!'

'School, Glorious School'

(to the tune of 'Food, Glorious Food' from *Oliver!*)

School, glorious school
Is it really vital?
It's not all that cool
And I'm feeling quite ill.

Reading, writing and algebra
What next? Not a maths test!
We're only here for one thing -
It's called recess!

'Mac!'

Mr Deery is looking straight at me. Along with the rest of the class.

'Uh, yeah?' I clearly missed something while *The Classroom Musical* was playing out in my head.

Mr Deery smiles at me. 'We all fully support your future rock career, but maybe we could save the humming of tunes for outside the classroom?'

I look around. Everyone's staring at me. Not in a mean way – most of them are smiling. I must have been humming pretty loud.

'Yeah, of course. Sorry, Mr Deery.'

'Don't be sorry. It was a pretty cool tune. Sounded familiar. What was it?'

I shrug. 'Dunno. Just something that was stuck in my head.' I'm not about to admit to the whole class that I was rewriting *Oliver!* and casting them all in the main performance.

'Alrighty then,' says Mr Deery, getting everyone's attention back to the front of the class. 'Back to adaptations. So the obvious example is from books to movies. Tyler mentioned Harry Potter. Any others?'

'Lemony Snicket,' says Isla.

'*Wonder*,' suggests Zeke.

'Great!' Mr Deery waves the rest of the hands down. 'How about a different kind of adaptation? When has a book been turned into something other than a movie?'

There's a pause, then Toma's hand goes up slowly.

'Toma?'

'*Frozen on Ice*?' he says.

Mr Deery's head rocks from side to side. 'Well, *Frozen* is a movie, not a book, but you're on the right track.'

'But my little sister has a *Frozen* book,' says Abby.

'Well, yes.' Mr Deery pinches the bridge of his nose. 'But originally it was a movie. That book is more like merchandise. So *Frozen on Ice* is actually a movie adaptation.'

'I don't get it,' says Abby.

'Me neither,' adds Toma.

'Okay,' says Mr Deery. 'I want you to try and think of a book where someone has taken the story and transformed it into something completely different. A different form of art. Maybe even in a way that is almost unrecognisable.'

Kids scrunch up their noses and look around at each other. Mr Deery waits patiently, looking out over the room of confusion.

'*West Side Story*,' I say, then clamp my hand over my mouth. How did that come out? Usually the Broadway stuff stays inside. Inside and quiet.

Mr Deery's head flicks up towards me. 'What was that?'

I try to avoid his eyes.

'Who said that?' he asks again.

Zeke points at me. 'Mac did.'

Gee, thanks, Zeke.

'What did you say, Mac?'

I slowly remove my hand from my mouth. 'Uh, I said, um, *West Side Story*?'

Mr Deery's eyes light up and he points at me like I've just reached the halfway mark on *Who Wants to Be a Millionaire*. 'Yes! Yes, exactly.'

'What's Western Story?' asks Isla.

'He said *West Side Story*,' corrects Abby.

Mr Deery waits for me to answer. I wait for him to.

'Go ahead, Mac,' he says, nodding towards me.

'Er, it's a musical.'

'What's a musical?' asks Connor.

'Like a play on stage, but with songs and dancing and stuff,' explains Cookie.

'Like *Frozen*!' says Toma.

'Sort of,' I explain. 'But *Frozen* is kinda just a movie with songs in it. Musicals are written especially for the stage and the songs tell the story.'

'And what is *West Side Story* an adaptation of, Mac?' Mr Deery asks.

'It's based on *Romeo and Juliet*, right?'

Mr Deery looks impressed. 'Sure is, Mac. Well done.' He turns back to face the class. 'Does everybody know the story of *Romeo and Juliet*?'

Some nods and mumbles come from the class.

'It's about looooooooooooove!' says Jesse, making a kissy face. Everyone laughs.

'Yes, well, we know it's about two people in love, but it's also about two people who come from families who are fighting and really don't like each other. And so their love is forbidden.' Mr Deery walks between the rows of our desks. '*West Side Story* took that same idea, but put it in a modern setting with two rival gangs on the streets of New York. So it's not just a straight adaptation, but they used the original story as an inspiration to say something new. It's an excellent example, Mac. Well done.'

I get that little gurgle in my tummy that happens when I get something right at school. It's a weird feeling but a nice one. It doesn't happen that often. I'm not bad at school, but I'm not great either – except in music class, with Ms Fox. That's where I feel at home. And today is Thursday, which means I get to spend the whole afternoon in the music room.

Mr Deery holds up the class iPad. 'All right, so I want you all to get in groups of four or five, and make a list of as many book adaptations as you can think of. Each group can use the iPad for fifteen minutes. Remember, it has to have been a book *first*, then turned into something else. Off you go.'

The mad rush of group selection starts. I just wait. No one ever really rushes to me but I also never get left out. All the best friends seize each other, then someone will grab me to make up the numbers.

'Mac, you wanna come with us?' asks Suruthi, clinging to her two best friends.

See.

'Sure,' I say, and head over to join them.

As they pounce on the iPad and start madly discussing their favourite books and movies, I let my mind drift off to what we might do in music class this afternoon.

The lunch bell rings and Suruthi hands our list to Mr Deery. I can't say I added too much but at least a couple of the titles on there came from me. I wait for the other kids to crush each other as they squeeze through the doorway then make my way between the desks.

'Mac?' Mr Deery stops me before I make it out. 'Do you have a minute?'

I don't have any lunchtime plans and give him a shrug to indicate that. 'Sure.' I lean on the corner of Mr Deery's desk. 'What's up, Mr D?' He smiles. I'm not being disrespectful. Mr D gets it. He doesn't mind that I call him Mr D. I think he kinda likes it.

'That was pretty cool how you knew about *West Side Story*, Mac.'

Cool? Knowing about Broadway? Maybe Mr D doesn't actually know what the word 'cool' means. I shrug again.

'Do you know any other musicals?' he asks me, his eyes narrowing slightly.

I've never talked to anyone about musicals before, except Ms Fox, and even she just humours me, I think. My eyes narrow back at him until we're like two newborn puppies squinting at each other. 'Maaaaaaybe,' I say slowly. 'Why?'

Mr Deery shrugs back. 'Well, maybe I do too.'

I pretend not to care, but I SO care. Another shrug. The shrugging is getting kind of ridiculous but it's hard to stop. 'So what?'

Mr Deery leans back in his chair and crosses his arms. 'So what if I said "Jellicles can"?'

Is this some kind of test? I know the answer, of course. I've listened to *Cats* a gazillion times. But nobody else knows that. I test the waters.

'I'd probably say "and Jellicles do".'

Mr Deery leans forward, elbows resting on his desk. 'Who's the head of the Pink Ladies?'

Please. Too easy.

'Rizzo.'

My teacher's eyes light up and a smile sneaks into the corner of his lips. 'And what about 24601?'

This time I don't hesitate. *Les Mis* is one of my all-time faves. 'Jean Valjean.'

Mr Deery seems satisfied. He grabs a pen and writes something down on a piece of paper, folding it four times and sliding it across the desk to me.

'I think you should join us tonight,' he says in a low voice. 'If your mum says it's okay. Maybe she could come too? Details are on the paper. The password is, "All that jazz".'

I pick up the paper. 'But what –'

'You are dismissed, Mac.'

'Huh?'

Mr Deery sighs. 'That means you can go.'

I watch Mr Deery as he pretends to go back to marking tests that haven't even been completed yet. 'You're being pretty weird, Mr D.'

'Thank you, Mac. Now off you go.'

I leave the classroom, confused and clutching the piece of paper tightly. I have no idea what's going on, but I like it.

Bolting down to the bottom oval, I find a quiet area to sit in, just next to the grassy banks. I slowly unfold the paper Mr Deery gave me and –

'Hey, Mac!'

I shove the paper into my pocket and look up to see Anishka Batan waving at me from the soccer field.

'We're about to start a game and we're short one,' she yells at me through cupped hands. 'You wanna join?'

I wave back. 'Nah, I'm good. Thanks, though.'

She shrugs, gives me a thumbs-up and runs off to find someone else. Alone again, I slowly unfold Mr D's piece of paper. Written at the top in capitals is . . .

SSOBMA

'Sob-ma?' I say to myself, sounding out the letters. 'What the . . .?'

I keep reading.

SECRET SOCIETY OF BROADWAY MUSICAL APPRECIATION. MEETING TODAY 4:00 PM BALTHAZAR THEATRE. REMEMBER THE PASSWORD.

I try to stay cool. I mean, there's, like, no reason to get excited about something your *teacher* invites you to, right? But I can't help it. My gut is floating around in my stomach like an astronaut blasted into space. There's a society? Who appreciate Broadway musicals? And it's SECRET? I feel like

Mr Deery heard all my wishes and scribbled them down on this torn piece of scrap paper.

Then the tummy-astronaut floats back down to Earth. Mum would never let me join a Broadway Musical Society. Plus I have band practice today – she'd kill me if I skipped it. I appreciate the thought, Mr D.

I fold the paper back up and tuck it carefully into my pocket. It's almost September, which means only four months until I turn twelve, and I *still* can't tell my mum that I don't wanna be a rock star. Maybe they teach courage in high school?

'Mac!'

It's Anishka again.

'Pleeeeeeeeease? We're still one short and I've got a packet of Twisties riding on this game.'

I jump to my feet. 'Yeah, sure thing.' I jog over to Anishka and she slaps me on the back.

'You're the best, Mac. Thanks!'

I join in the soccer game and try my best to help Anishka win the Twisties, but the fact is, there's only one thing on my mind . . .

SSOBMA!

ACT ONE
Scene Three

Ms Fox's Music Room

A chaotic music room. Kids sit at different instruments - plonking away on xylophones, tapping bongos, tooting the odd recorder - all waiting for their music teacher, who is never on time. As the kids play, they begin to sing . . .

'We've Got to Sing a Song or Two'

(to the tune of 'You've Got to Pick a Pocket or Two' from *Oliver!*)

Why must we, always wait
For our teacher, always late
Unpack the shelves, we'll teach ourselves
We've got to sing a song or two.
We've got to sing a song or two, kids.
We've got to sing a song or two.

We know what Ms Fox would do
We've got to sing a song or two.
(Let's show her how we do it, my peers!)

Pluck guitar, hit a drum
Music class, so much fun
Volume goes up, when she turns up
We've got to sing a song or two.
We've got to sing a song or two, kids.
We've got to sing a song or two.

'I'm sorry, kids!' Ms Fox rushes in, stuff falling out of her bag, a guitar strap wrapped around her neck. Our class has music the same time every Thursday, but it still always manages to be a surprise to Ms Fox.

She tries to take her bag off, but the bag strap is under the guitar strap and she ends up tangling herself in, well, everything. We watch as she hops around the front of the room, trying to remove herself from the mess she's created. She pulls her arm out of one of her sleeves, her leather jacket now half covering her head. Ms Fox has been in the classroom for exactly 45 seconds (after being ten minutes late) and she already needs my help. I put down my guitar and walk over to get her out of her accessory maze.

'Stop wiggling!' I say, trying to pull her bag back over her left arm.

'I'm not wiggling!' says Ms Fox, wiggling some more.

'Just sit down, Ms Fox.' I guide her over to a chair, and me and three other kids finally manage to get her out of her mess.

'Thanks, everyone! So, you ready?'

I laugh. We're always ready; she never is. But she has a teacher persona to try to keep up so we let it slide.

She adjusts her guitar and settles in. 'Let's start with some Blink-182. Grab something to hit – preferably not each other. Let's warm up by rockin' out.'

Everyone rushes for the instruments. In the end there's only a güiro left. It's the thing that kinda looks like a wooden fish with bumps that you play with a stick. I'm not fussed. I grab it and take my seat on the floor.

Ms Fox looks at me and shakes her head. 'Go grab your guitar, Mac.'

'I'm fine, seriously,' I say. I don't like getting special treatment in music class, even though I'm pretty sure I'm Ms Fox's favourite.

'Kids! Does anyone mind if Mac plays guitar?'

Everyone makes rock hands and yells, 'Rock on, Mac!'

In Ms Fox's class, we're not allowed to sit up straight or raise our hands or stand in line. Ms Fox says those are school rules. In this room we follow rock rules. The first thing you learn is 'rock hands' – pinky and index fingers raised. Ms Fox says if she sees anyone in her class raise their hand, it MUST be a rock hand.

'The people have spoken,' says Ms Fox. I smile and put the güiro back. I take my guitar out of its case. There are no left-handed ones in the classroom so I always get to use mine.

'Amp or no amp?' asks Ms Fox.

Rock hands all round. 'AMP!'

'As you wish.' Ms Fox plugs in and invites me to join her. I plug in next to her.

'"All the Small Things"?' I ask.

She nods and counts us in . . .

'Five, six, seven, eight.'

Our guitars pump through the speakers and the kids in class bang out the driving beat. We all know the words and sing along. It's a class favourite. When the *'na-na, na-na'* comes in, everyone's on their feet, jumping around the classroom, singing at the top of their voices. Ms Fox lets me take the breakdown solo as Mia Ledden builds the crescendo on the full drum kit.

We rewrote some of the lyrics at the beginning of the year and we scream them out loud, not worrying if we're in tune.

`Long day, come home. School sucks, I know!`

Only Ms Fox would let us say that. But she says everyone has days that suck, including kids. And singing about it can be . . . what did she call it? Therapeutic!

Rocking out feels so good, so freeing. Like all your worries are exploding out of your body. Every kid in this room is rockin' like no one's watching. Especially Ms Fox. Her hair whips around her head as she jumps and jams. We all sing louder.

```
I dump my school bag by the stairs,
got homework but you know, who cares!
```

I feel the excitement build as it gets to everyone's favourite bit . . .

```
Minecraft to play, Mum says, 'No way!'
I hear her boom, 'CLEAN UP YOUR ROOM!'
```

We all jump in unison, singing . . .

```
NA-NA, NA-NA, NA-NA, NA-NA, NA, NA!
```

BANG! The door bursts open. Mrs Keiren stands in the doorway, hands on hips, face like the angry emoji. The music screeches to a halt. 'What on Earth is going on here?' she screams.

Principal Keiren is wearing a shirt with lace ruffles around her neck. A red flush is rising out of the collar and spreading into her face like a volcano. Ever since the prank earlier this year where Casey Wu put a chicken alarm clock under her chair, all the kids have started calling her 'Principal Chicken'. Wearing a ruffled collar is really not helping her cause.

We all look to Ms Fox, who's trying to get her mane of hair out of her mouth and off her face. 'Ah, um, we were just . . .' She splutters a little, trying to spit out the remaining hairs and pat her 'do' back into something semi-respectable. '. . . warming up,' she explains.

'I could hear that commotion from the science block,' growls the principal.

Ms Fox takes the guitar strap off from around her neck. 'It's not commotion,' she says. 'It's music.'

'Well, that's a matter of opinion,' says Mrs Keiren, raising her eyebrows and screwing up her nose like she just smelled one of Stevie's farts.

Ms Fox sighs. 'No, actually, it's not. The literal definition of music is vocal or instrumental sounds, or in our case both, to produce an expression of emotion. And what were we expressing, kids?'

'Frustration!'

'Joy!'

'A love of rock!'

Casey Wu smiles at Mrs Keiren. 'Indignation.'

I don't even know what that means. Casey always uses words I don't understand. But it seems to make Mrs Kieran flare up like a frill-necked lizard.

'Well, I – and the rest of the school, who are trying to get an education – would prefer if you reduced the volume and perhaps kept to the curriculum?'

I can tell Ms Fox is trying not to laugh. 'We will do our very best, Mrs Keiren. Any particular requests?'

Mrs Keiren glares at us all, then points to a Beethoven poster on the wall. 'Why don't you try some real music, like Beethoven? Maybe you will actually learn something!'

'Great idea!' says Ms Fox. 'Gather round, kids, and let me play you a little tune.'

Ms Fox plugs her iPod into the amp and flicks through her music. 'Here's a song I think you're going to love.' She presses play and dramatic strings blast through the speaker. Content with herself, Mrs Keiren heads back towards the door.

'This disco masterpiece, inspired by Beethoven's "Symphony No. 5", was on the *Saturday Night Fever* soundtrack in 1977. The genius of Walter Murphy shows that with a little musical flair, you can breathe life into even the stuffiest of sorts.' Ms Fox aims that last comment at Mrs Keiren's back, just before she leaves the room.

At that same moment, a funky disco beat kicks into the song and the principal spins around.

Ms Fox smiles. 'All right, kids, show me your disco moves!'

Everyone in the room breaks into their best disco-boogie. I bust out my classic funky-chicken as Mrs Keiren huffs, shakes her head and walks out the door, leaving Ms Fox to have her wonderfully terrible influence on us.

The song comes to an end and we are all boogied out. 'All right, everyone, grab a ukulele and let's see if we can get through the first verse and chorus of "I'm Yours" by Jason Mraz.'

Ms Fox puts the chords chart up on the board and we all settle down on the floor with our ukuleles. 'Pass around your music journals,' she says, handing the colourful books to the kids at the front, who find their own and pass the rest back. Most kids get one journal for the whole school year. I'm on my fifth. But Ms Fox doesn't mind. She says any music in our minds should go in the book. I guess there's just a lot of music in my head.

As Ms Fox runs us through the chords we've already learnt and the strumming patterns for the song, a calm settles over the room. Anyone who doesn't believe in the magic of music should just take a look at the power Ms Fox and her ukuleles have over this normally unruly bunch of eleven-year-olds.

I've been learning guitar since I was four, so these ukulele class jams are super easy for me, but that doesn't mean I enjoy them any less. I help the other kids with the fingering on their chords and rewrite some of the song lyrics in my head. Not that Jason Mraz hasn't done a good job. Just, sometimes I like to change the words around a little so they have more meaning for me. I mean, look, I'm only in Year Six. I haven't been in love yet and a lot (like a *lot*) of songs are about love and smooshy stuff like that. Sometimes I just like to bring the words a little closer to my own life. I scribble down the new lyrics in my journal.

```
So I won't clean my bedroom floor, no more
        Homework can wait, I'm sure.
```

I think about the long to-do list of boring tasks that wait for me at home and the lyrics flow out of me and onto the page.

```
    There's no need to brush my teeth,
           my chores are blah
       This is my point, I'm bored.
```

Music class goes by way too fast for my liking, and before I know it, the bell is ringing for us to finish up.

'Instruments away, rock stars, and everyone pass their music journals back to the front.'

The others dump their stuff back in the racks and toss the journals into the box. I hang back a bit and tidy up the mess, making sure the ukuleles are lined up properly and straightening the pile of journals.

Everyone funnels out of the classroom but Ms Fox stops Mia Ledden.

'Mia, Mac. I'm really sorry, but I'm going to have to move band practice from this afternoon – is that okay?'

Mia shrugs. 'Yeah, sure.'

'Can you let your sister know? How are you getting home?'

'Yep, no worries. Bee is on her way here now from Ms McKay's class, so we'll just grab the bus instead like we usually do. Dad's at home so it makes no difference to us.'

'Great, I'll give him a call too. I've let Toby know. How about you, Mac?'

'I walk home anyway, so it's all the same to me,' I say.

'Thought so. Want me to text your mum?'

'It's okay. I'll do it.'

Mia points through the window in the music room doors. Bee's face is pushed up against the glass. 'There's Bee now. I'll tell her. See ya, Ms Fox.'

'Bye, Mia. And be sure to thank Bee for the nostril prints on my window.'

Mia laughs and heads out the door, grabbing her twin sister on the way. Mia and Bee Ledden make up half of our band, The Ants Pants. Mia plays drums and Bee plays bass guitar. I'm on lead guitar and Toby Baker from Year 5 is our lead vocalist. He's just a small kid but wow can he sing!

I untangle the mass of xylophone sticks that are piled up in the corner.

'You don't have to do that, Mac. I've got it. One of the joys of being a music teacher.' Ms Fox grins at me.

I grin back but continue to help. 'I didn't think there were any.'

She laughs. 'Just that one. But seriously, you can go home.'

I shrug. 'I wasn't supposed to be home till later anyway 'cos of band, so it's no worries.'

'Okay then, your call. Should we at least work to some tunes? I'll even let you choose.'

'Definitely,' I say, jumping up and heading over to Ms Fox's iPod. I flick through her playlists. A little warm feeling of pride bubbles in my stomach as I see 'Mac's faves' among others like 'Chill out', 'Songs to sing into a hairbrush' and 'Driving on the wrong side of the road'.

'So did you listen?' I ask.

Ms Fox nods.

The warm feeling in my stomach flips a switch into hollow as the pride turns into nerves. What if she hated the Broadway playlist I put together for her? I mean, I've never actually heard Ms Fox say that she hates ANY music but she's also never played us any stuff from musicals in class. She might hate it. She probably hated it. Will she think I'm weird for liking it? Will she kick me out of the band? I mean it's a rock band, after all. There's no room for a musical theatre lover, right?

'Some of it was pretty cool,' she says, rolling up the chord chart. I let out the breath I didn't even know I'd been holding and the warm, bubbly feeling comes back. Ms Fox turns, pointing the rolled-up poster at me. 'I really like the Pharaoh song from that Joseph and his jacket one. What's it called?'

'*Joseph and the Amazing Technicolor Dreamcoat*,' I answer.

She laughs. 'Yeah, that's it. Ridiculous name, great songs.'

'Andrew Lloyd Webber is a genius. And don't even get me started on Tim Rice. One of the best lyricists in the business.'

'Cool.'

I'm beaming. Cool? No one I know has ever thought musical theatre was cool before. Especially not someone as actually cool as Ms Fox. I pull the folded-up paper from my pocket and look at it again.

SSOBMA.

I check my watch. It's only 3:40 pm. I could still make it. I roll the paper between my finger and thumb, unsure of what to do.

Ms Fox looks up at me. 'Hey, Mac. What if we did a lesson on Broadway? We could maybe learn a song or two, look at the different kinds of musicals – maybe even talk about the difference between lyrics of a pop song and those of musical numbers in the way they tell a story.'

I stare at her. 'Seriously?'

She shrugs. 'Sure, why not? I always like to interpret the syllabus creatively anyway.' She winks at me. 'Plus you know my theory – all music is good music, love what you love. And I reckon if a little dude like you digs this stuff so much then we should share it around. What do you think?'

'I . . . I would love that,' I say softly.

'Sweet,' says Ms Fox. 'You'd better make me another playlist then.'

I take one more look at the paper and tuck it back into my pocket. 'Absolutely,' I say, jumping to my feet. 'Hey, Ms Fox, I gotta run, but I'll give you some more songs tomorrow.'

'Okay, Mac, check ya! And get ready for Broadway 101, thanks to Mac Cooper.'

I pause at the door and turn over my shoulder. 'Hey, Ms Fox,' I say quietly.

She looks up from the bag that she's packing. 'Yeah?'

I stare down at my feet. 'Maybe don't tell anyone that it was my idea?'

'Why not?'

I shrug.

'I see. Got a rock-star reputation to maintain, do we?'

I don't answer and stay looking at my shoes.

Ms Fox sighs. 'Okay, Mac, whatever. But you're the one who made me listen to "Expressing Yourself" from *Billy Elliot*. Maybe you should have another listen yourself?'

I don't look at her. Easy for her to say. Bet her mum doesn't wear t-shirts declaring what kind of music is acceptable.

'Mac.'

I look up and she smiles that Ms Fox smile that kinda just makes everything okay. 'I've emailed you a new song. I haven't finished yet – I'm still going to add some more bass – but it's enough for you to start on the lyrics.'

I grin and give her a double thumbs-up. 'You bet.'

Ms Fox writes songs. Like really cool songs. I don't know why she's teaching us, she could totally be a professional. I asked her once and she said, 'I *am* a professional. A professional music teacher.' That wasn't what I meant but I let it slide. And the best part is she lets me write the lyrics for her songs. Me! Some little eleven-year-old kid. And she seems to actually like them. That or she's really good at pretending.

I like playing guitar, but I *really* like writing lyrics. I don't like to dream too big because I know it'll probably never happen but sometimes, when I'm lying in bed and I sort of lose control of my thoughts, I think about how I'd love to write my very own Broadway musical. Dumb, huh? Seriously, Watterson couldn't be any further from Broadway if it tried.

The clock behind Ms Fox's head catches my eye. 3:45 pm. If I'm going to go to the SSOBMA meeting, I gotta jet.

'Better run, Ms Fox. See ya tomorrow?'

'You bet, kiddo. Stay cool.' She gives me a fist bump and I head out of the music room. Pausing in the hallway, I pull out my phone to text Mum.

Hey Mum. Band practice has been cancelled but Mr Deery asked me to

I pause, thinking about the best way to put this.

join another music group. Is that okay? They meet at Balthazar Theatre after school. I'll still be home same time.

A few seconds pass and Mum texts back.

Music group? Like another band?

I'm not sure what to do here. I definitely don't want to lie to her. I decide to go with something reassuring, yet non-committal.

☺

She texts back straight away.

Sounds awesome! Have fun and say hi to Mr D for me. Text when you leave AND when you get home. X

You bet. Thanks Mum. X

And before you can say 'The Schuyler Sisters', I'm out the school gate and halfway down Aruma Road on my way to Balthazar Theatre.

ACT ONE
Scene Four

Balthazar Theatre

Outside Balthazar Theatre, Mac hesitates, not sure if he is making the right move. He goes to knock on the door and stops. Paces back and forth, looking at his watch, looking at the crumpled piece of paper. He goes to knock again and stops . . . again!

'I Gotta Join SSOBMA'

(to the tune of 'Hakuna Matata' from *The Lion King*)

I gotta join SSOBMA
They're a musical team.
I gotta join SSOBMA
The acronym is extreme.

I just gotta knock
And finally realise my dream.

It is waiting for me
A musical community.
I gotta join SSOBMA.

Mac takes a deep breath and finally knocks on the door.

I look at my hand. Did it just knock on its own? I don't know if I'm ready to . . .

'Can I help you, hon?'

A blonde woman stands in the doorway looking at me like I've just been dropped there by an alien spaceship – which is exactly how I feel.

'Um, I – I, er . . . I'm here for . . .' Yup, I want to write songs and THIS is how good I am at words.

She gives me a kind smile. 'We're between shows at the moment, honey. You can check the website for upcoming performances.'

I shake my head. 'No, I'm here for the . . .' Come on, words, where are you? Then I remember the password. 'All that jazz!' I blurt out.

She laughs. 'Ah ha! You're here for the Broadway group.' She opens the door wide and waves her hand dramatically through the opening. 'Well, come on in then.'

I walk through the doors and into the theatre. 'Wow!' It's just like I imagined a theatre would be. A big foyer with old but fancy carpet leading to giant wooden doors that probably open up to a stage and tiered seating. There are huge pillars and big posters of past shows. It's exactly like *42nd Street*. 'This is so cool.'

The lady smiles at me. 'Yes, well, I think so. Have you never been here before?'

'Nah. We're not really a theatre kind of family.'

She laughs. 'Well, I'm not sure there's such a thing, but my kids would be happy to swap families if you're keen?'

I think she's making a joke, so I smile politely, but mostly I'm just looking around, trying to soak up every little bit of the theatre and print it into my memory. It's hard to believe that Watterson has a place as cool as this.

The lady looks at me, probably expecting me to say something, but I just tilt my head back to take in the domed roof.

'I'm Jennifer Heckleston, the Operations Manager here at Balthazar Theatre.' She looks at me expectantly, but I've got nothing. 'And you are?'

Right! My name. Of course.

'Sorry. I'm Mac Cooper. Mr Deery invited me here.'

'Of course. Do you go to Watterson Primary?'

I nod. I'm trying to focus on Ms Heckleston and the conversation, but there's a *Phantom of the Opera* poster on the wall behind her.

'My daughters go there too. Tess might be around your age. Tess Heckleston, do you know her?'

A laugh escapes before I realise how rude that is and cover my mouth. Everyone knows Tess Heckleston. She may not be in my year, but it's hard not to know about the kid who found a million bucks and took down an actual real-life criminal.

Ms Heckleston sighs. 'Yes, of course you do. Who doesn't know my infamous daughter?'

'Sorry, Ms Heckleston. But yeah, kind of everyone knows her.'

'Please, just Jennifer.' She waves at me to follow her. 'That offer of a family swap is still open if you change your mind?'

I'm pretty sure Tess has about four siblings. Stevie alone is a big enough handful. 'Thanks,' I say. 'I'll, um, think about it.'

I follow Jennifer through the foyer. I can't even imagine how cool it would be to have a mum that works here. Being able to hang out and play on the stage and see all the shows you want – for free! I've been to the pub Mum works at – The Garage. It's hot, it smells and, if there's no live band playing, it's super boring. I'd give anything for my mum to work here instead.

Jennifer pushes on the heavy wooden double doors and I can almost hear the DA, DAAAAH! in my head as the gorgeous theatre inside is revealed. Burgundy velvet-covered seats sit in semi-circles facing a giant stage framed by plush red curtains. Lights line the walls and ceiling, highlighting the decorative patterns in the plaster and wood.

‘Wow!’ I say again.

‘Yes, well, it’s getting a bit old and definitely needs some work, but it’s home.’ Jennifer smiles warmly and points to a small group of people gathered in front of the stage. ‘Those are your people down there. Have fun, hon.’ She pats me on the shoulder and walks back through the doors, closing them and leaving me standing by myself in the huge theatre.

Suddenly, I’m not sure this is such a great idea. Maybe if I turn around and slowly creep back out those doors, Jennifer might let me wander around and look at the posters for a bit and I could just –

‘Mac!’

Mr Deery’s waving at me from down front. ‘Come and join us.’

Too late to leave now. I take a deep breath and walk down the aisle towards him.

My eyes adjust to the dim theatre light as I get closer. Walking slowly, I scan the group before I reach them. This is the strangest bunch of people I’ve ever seen. Every size, shape and age . . . except mine. I’m the youngest here by at least a hundred years. Okay, maybe twenty, but that's still a lot. I'm regretting this now. I should've known no young people would be in a Broadway appreciation society. I'm the only weirdo my age who likes musical theatre. I want to turn and bolt, but my feet keep moving forward.

Mr Deery throws his arms into the air. 'Mac! I'm so glad you came. I wasn't sure you would, to be honest.'

I force a smile like I don't know what he's talking about. 'Of course, Mr D.'

'And you told your mum where you are?'

Sometimes Mr D can be *such* a teacher. 'I thought you said it was a *secret* society?'

Mr Deery crosses his arms. 'Secret like exclusive, not secret like you don't still need your mum's permission.'

I take out my phone and open Mum's texts, turning the screen towards Mr Deery.

'Great! Let me introduce you to the crew.'

I'm pretty sure Mr Deery is trying to make the group sound cooler by calling them a 'crew', but I see straight through it.

'This here is Giuseppe.' He points at an old guy sitting on some sort of chair with handles and wheels, looking at a stack of papers and mumbling to himself. 'Giuseppe, this is our newest member, Mac.'

I put my hands up. 'I don't know if I can be a member yet. You know, with band practice and babysitting my little brother and schoolwork. I just came to, like, check it out.'

Mr Deery nods. 'Of course. Well, this is still Giuseppe.' The man looks up and gives me a smile filled with the whitest, straightest, squarest false teeth I've ever seen. I'm almost blinded by the theatre lights bouncing off them and directly into my eyeballs.

'Why, hello there, young man.' Giuseppe puts his hands on the sides of his chair and slowly pushes himself to his feet. He shuffles around, grabbing the contraption by the handles, and pushes it towards me, closing the gap, agonisingly slow step by agonisingly slow step. It occurs to me halfway through that it would have been much easier (and much more polite) for me to have gone over to him, but he's almost here now and I don't want to break his flow.

After what feels like forever, he finally reaches me. Clocking up record speeds of about ten minutes per metre. I feel a bit bad but Giuseppe looks quite chuffed with himself. 'Nice to meet you, Mac.' He reaches out a wrinkled hand. 'Is that short for something?'

I take his hand and shake it gently. 'No, sir. Just Mac.'

Giuseppe lets go of my hand and takes hold of his walker again. He spins it around like a dance move and sits back down. There's something almost graceful about the way he gets around. It's kind of calming to watch and to wait for him.

'I like it,' says Giuseppe, once he's settled back down. 'Like "Mack the Knife".'

I look at him blankly.

'Bobby Darin?'

Nothing.

'Shark bites? Pearly whites?'

Nope.

'*The Threepenny Opera*?'

Blank.

Giuseppe shakes his head at me. 'Thank goodness you joined us. So much to learn.'

Mr Deery turns me towards a lady in a business suit, tapping furiously on her phone, her thumbs moving at the speed of light. Her dark hair is pulled back severely from her face and her eyebrows furrow in the middle as she stares at the screen.

'And this is Binita,' says Mr Deery, waving his hand at her expectantly.

Binita barely moves, just raising one finger to indicate that we should wait while continuing to tap fluidly with the other thumb. I look around the group as they watch her finish off whatever she's writing. If nothing else, I will certainly learn patience from these people. She presses what I assume is send and then lifts her head to face me. A brilliant smile paints across her face and her eyes dance, completely transforming her appearance. It's hard to believe this is the same harsh-looking woman who was emailing (or maybe playing Candy Crush?) with such intensity two seconds ago.

She sings at me in a voice that echoes through the theatre with intense vibrato.

'Hellooooooo!'

She waits for the echo to die down, looking very pleased with her efforts. 'The name is Binita.' She gazes up at the ceiling, waving jazz hands theatrically over imaginary stars. 'Lawyer by day, triple threat by night.'

I extend my hand like Giuseppe did. 'Nice to meet you.'

She looks at my hand like it's covered in walrus snot. 'No, I don't shake,' she says. She smiles once more and turns back to her phone.

Mr Deery shakes his head and turns up towards the stage. I follow his gaze, raising my hand in front of my eyes to try and block out some glare from the stage lights. I squint and dodge my head but all I can see is a silhouette holding a guitar.

'And this character you most likely already know.'

The figure moves forward on the stage, stepping in front of the lights, and grins down at me. 'Kathy, musical maestro, at your service!' she announces, strumming a few chords of 'Razzle Dazzle' from *Chicago*.

'Have you two met?' asks Mr Deery.

'Sort of,' I say. 'I helped build her Lego house in Brennan Park. Twice, in fact!'

'And I am very grateful to you,' says Kathy, giving a little bow. Her pet ferret, Mr Piddles, scurries around her neck to stop from slipping off as she bends over. When she straightens up, he settles back into his usual spot on her shoulder. 'And of course I know Mac, resident child rock star; big brother of Stevie; son of Nicole Cooper, also known as Nikki, who works at The Garage; and they all live on . . . Merricks Road, from memory.'

I stare at Kathy. She stares back.

Mr Deery sighs. 'You know it's kind of creepy when you do that, Kathy?'

'Kind of?' I say. 'How do you know all that?'

Kathy taps her finger to her temple. 'All up here,' she says proudly. 'More info than a *Yellow Pages* in this noggin.'

'What's a *Yellow Pages*?'

Kathy huffs. 'Nothin' but a doorstop these days with your fancy Google search. But it used to tell us everything about this town. Now you can just look it up in the Kathy Pages.'

She laughs at her own joke and Mr Deery and I share a sideways glance. She catches the look.

'Not happy, Jan!' With that she turns away, strumming her guitar and singing to herself.

I whisper to Mr Deery. 'Is she . . .?'

'A wealth of musical knowledge? Yes.' Mr Deery leans down. 'You might be surprised what you can learn from her, Mac. She's been playing guitar for longer than you've been alive.'

I scoff a little. I don't want to sound stuck-up or anything, but I just finished learning the guitar solo from 'Stairway to Heaven'. I'm pretty sure I couldn't look that up in her 'Kathy Pages' or whatever it was called.

I look around the theatre. 'Is that it?' I ask. 'Is that all of you?' I'm not sure what I expected, but I'm definitely disappointed. I think I was hoping for the audition scene from *A Chorus Line* – fifty people lined up in sweats, performing choreographed dances while an arrogant (but charming) director counts out loud and yells at them to point their toes and give him jazz hands. Instead, I got . . . this. I don't even really know what 'this' is.

Mr Deery sees the doubt in my face.

'There's one more,' he says, smiling reassuringly. 'Another kid your age. Well, a year older. I think you guys are going to –'

The doors burst open. 'Sorry I'm gherkin late, everybody. Wheeee! My gherkin teacher held me back again. Stop!'

A kid runs down the aisle, backpack bouncing up and down, arms full of papers, a few of which tumble to the ground behind him. He halts, turns around to pick them up and then continues towards us. He stops in front of us and thrusts the papers at Mr Deery.

'Here's the sheet gherkin music for next week. Ms Toor says next time you wheeee, stop have to do the gherkin copying yourself. Copyright the floss dance move!'

Mr Deery smiles and takes the papers. The boy gives Mr Deery a peace sign and turns to me.

'Who's this gherkin?'

Did he just call me a gherkin? Is that even an insult? His arm flicks up to give me a quick thumbs-up. Maybe it's a compliment?

Mr Deery smiles. 'Flynn, this is Mac. Mac, Flynn.'

'Hi,' I say.

'Wheeee hi,' says Flynn. He points to the sky and I look up, but see nothing except the roof. 'Are you gherkin joining the team? Stop.'

I turn to Mr Deery but he just nods towards Flynn.

'I'm just checking it out,' I say.

'Cool.' Flynn walks over to the piano and dumps his bag on the stool. 'Do you wheeee, gherkin play an instrument? Play a dog whistle. Gherkin.'

'Yeah, um, guitar.' I step closer. 'Sorry, but did you say "gherkin"?'

Flynn stares at me, confused. 'No, did you?' His chest does a little bounce like he's holding in a hiccup and he gives me a peace sign. I look around at the others in the group. Everyone just stares back at me.

'But . . . but I swear you said . . .'

Flynn's chest bounces once more. I think he's holding his breath. Then he lets go. 'Gherkin, wheeee, stop!' He laughs, and everyone else joins in.

'I couldn't hold it in any gherkin longer. The look on your gherkin face stop. Face like a cat's bum.'

I am so, *so* confused. Flynn walks over and puts his hand on my shoulder. 'I've got gherkin Tourette's syndrome, little dude. You know what that stop is? Wheeee!'

I shake my head.

'It's a brain thing that gherkin gives me tics stop. Which means I make whoop movements and shout gherkin gherkin gherkin without choosing to. So if you're gonna wheeee hang out with us stop, then there are a couple of gherkin things you're going to have to whoop get used to.'

Flynn sits me down in a chair. 'Here's the gherkin rundown. Mr Deery is supposed to wheeee be in charge gherkin, but he's too nice to organise anything whoop.'

Mr Deery shrugs, throwing his hands up in the air to indicate there's nothing he can do about it.

'Giuseppe gherkin takes a long time to wheeee get anywhere but he'll out-sing gherkin anyone.'

Giuseppe smiles modestly and lifts his hat a little. Flynn gives another thumbs-up. 'Your teeth hurt my eyeball brain!'

I look at Giuseppe but he doesn't seem to be offended. I mean, his teeth *are* super white.

Flynn continues, unfazed. 'If you can get Binita off her gherkin phone call the Batphone, she lights up the gherkin stage.' Binita rolls her eyes and flicks her hair before returning to her phone.

'Kathy is a little unpredictable gherkin, and that's coming from me stop. Whoop.'

I turn to Kathy. She doesn't seem to be listening.

'And me? Wheeee. Well, with me gherkin, you have to get used to a few stop things. Firstly, the word gherkin gherkin. A few excited sounds like wheeee and whoop stop. And then of course stop. Which doesn't actually mean gherkin I want you to stop wheeee!'

I just sit there. This is a lot to take in. Flynn's arm jerks up and he gives me rock hands.

I point. 'What was that?' Then, realising how rude I'm being, I snap my arm back down again. 'Sorry,' I say, staring into my lap.

'Don't be gherkin sorry,' says Flynn. 'I also have whoop a motor tic in my gherkin left arm, so you'll wheeee see any combination of thumbs-up gherkin, peace sign, rock hands stop and sometimes gherkin even the rude finger. That one can gherkin get me into a bit of wheeee trouble. The oyster is a pinecone's cousin.'

'And that?'

Flynn shrugs. 'Then there are just gherkin some randoms whoop. You'll get stop used to it.' Flynn claps his hands. 'Okay gherkin, great. Any more questions wheeee?'

Everyone looks at me. Any more questions? I have so many questions. Like so, so, **SO** many questions.

I shake my head. 'Nope.'

'Great wheeee, whoop, let's get gherkin started stop.'

Flynn takes a seat at the piano and shuffles some music on the stand. 'Wheeee, whoop, stop!' His arm flings a paper off the stand. He picks it up and replaces it. 'What's gherkin first?'

Mr Deery gathers everyone around the piano. We wait patiently for Giuseppe as he moves his walker. Flynn's tics continue. 'Gherkin, wheeee, stop.' I listen to the rhythm of his tics. It sounds a little like the beginning of 'Cell Block Tango'.

There's something quite musical to it.

'What does everyone want to start with?' asks Mr Deery.

Giuseppe opens his mouth. '"Bring him – "'

Binita pounces on him. 'I swear if you suggest *Les Mis* one more time, I will pull that walker out from under you!'

'Binita!' scolds Mr Deery.

You would think Mr Deery gets enough of telling kids off at school, but here he is doing it with big kids in his free time too. Sucker for punishment, I guess.

Binita rolls her eyes. 'Like anyone else wants to hear his Jean Valjean for the hundredth time. Let's do *Wicked*! Maybe "Defying Gravity"? I'm happy to take the role of Elphaba.'

Kathy interjects. 'That's a solo, Binita. Maybe we could try an ensemble number so everyone can join in.'

'How about gherkin first timer's choice whoop?' suggests Flynn, gesturing to me.

'Great idea,' agrees Mr Deery. 'Mac? What do you want to do?'

All eyes are on me. I shrug.

'Well, son – what's your favourite musical?' asks Giuseppe.

I shrug again.

Binita looks at me in horror. 'You can't very well join if you don't have a favourite musical,' she scoffs.

Flynn glares at her. 'Who made you the gherkin queen of rules, Binita? Whoop!' He turns back to me. 'Do you have a gherkin favourite, Mac wheeee? Mac and cheese.'

I look up at Flynn and he gives me a thumbs-up. I'm not sure if it's a tic or encouragement, but either way it makes me smile.

'*Hairspray*,' I say.

'Yes!' yells Mr Deery. 'Which song?'

I grin. 'Maybe "You Can't Stop the Beat"?'

'Whoop! Stop. Yes, I love playing that gherkin.' Flynn pulls out a folder and flips through his music. 'Wheeee! Stop. "You Can't Stop the Beat". I can beat you in a sack race.' He grins at me. 'Getting wheeee excited makes me gherkin tic even more, and I LOVE this whoop song stop.' Flynn's arm flicks up, giving me a peace sign.

I wonder how on Earth this is going to work. How can Flynn possibly play the piano with his tics, and how are we going to sing over the top of all those 'gherkins'? I look around but nobody else seems fazed. They all pull out their own folders.

'Do you want to share mine?' asks Kathy.

'Oh, I sort of know the words already,' I say quietly.

'Very impressive,' says Kathy. 'I can't remember my own name most days.'

Flynn carefully straightens the music on the piano once, twice and then a third time. 'Whoop! Gherkin. Gherkin. Stop!' Kathy walks over to him and places Mr Piddles on the piano seat. The ferret scuttles up onto Flynn's leg and curls up in his lap. Flynn stops rearranging the music and slowly strokes Mr Piddles.

'Who's playing who?' asks Giuseppe.

Mr Deery runs his finger down the page. 'How about Mac, you take Tracy's part? Giuseppe, you be Link. Binita and I will be Penny and Seaweed. And Kathy, you do Edna.'

'And I'll pick up the gherkin Corny Collins lines wheeee!' says Flynn.

'Perfect,' agrees Mr Deery.

The doubt on my face must be obvious because Flynn grins at me. 'I'll stick to the gherkin lyrics, I promise stop!' He gives me one last peace sign and turns to the piano.

Flynn takes a deep breath and then, as he exhales softly, his fingers dance gracefully across the keys. His foot taps the pedals as the melody of the piano fills the theatre. My mouth drops open. His hands bounce lightly as his fingers cross over each other so fast, it's almost a blur. It's so effortless and beautiful. Ms Fox would love this kid. She always says we gotta let go when we play, and Flynn . . . he really lets go.

Suddenly he stops. Everyone's looking at me again.

'You missed your gherkin cue wheeee!' says Flynn.

'I – I'm sorry,' I say. 'You're just so good.'

Flynn grins. 'Thanks stop! No, don't stop, that was a whoop tic. I like gherkin compliments. Tell me I'm the king of sweatpants.'

'But . . . but you don't tic when you play?'

Flynn shrugs and give me rock hands. 'Yeah, I dunno gherkin. It's a thing for me wheeee. Concentrating on playing keeps my stop brain busy and the focusing sort of whoop makes me tic less for a bit. Doesn't gherkin work for everybody with stop Tourette's wheeee, but for me it does. Piano is just my jam, I gherkin guess. Whoop!'

'Let's try again?' suggests Mr Deery.

I nod.

'Don't let me wheeee down this time gherkin, Mac,' threatens Flynn jokingly.

A deep breath and his fingers dance again. It's mesmerising. But not so much that I miss my cue. I come in right on time and Flynn grins.

The theatre fills with music and singing and joy as I jam along with these new . . . friends, I guess. I have this weird feeling. It's a calm feeling. Like I can just be me: Mac, musical enthusiast. Perhaps even: Mac, newest member of SSOBMA.

'So what do you think?' asks Mr Deery as he packs up the chairs. 'Will we see you again?'

The last hour has pretty much been the best fun I've had . . . ever! I can't even pretend I'm thinking about it. 'For sure!'

'Gherkin. Awesome! Power to the sheepdog.' Flynn rests his elbow on my shoulder. 'It'll be nice to whoop have some more gherkin young blood in this stop ancient society.'

'Hey! Easy, tiger,' warns Mr Deery.

I give him a hand with stacking the chairs. 'Can I ask – why is it a secret society? Doesn't really seem necessary?'

Binita, who is not helping at all with the pack-up but rather typing another essay on her phone, answers without looking up. 'My musical career and my law career must be kept separate. Can't have one undermining the other.'

'And I'm already having enough trouble fighting off the ladies.' Giuseppe flashes his glowing grin at me. 'Imagine if they knew I could sing and dance as well?'

Kathy strokes Mr Piddles. 'I like anything that's underground. It adds a certain je ne sais quoi to the experience.'

'A certain what?' I ask.

'Exactly!' she says, and walks away.

'We just like to surround ourselves with like minds,' explains Mr Deery.

I turn to Flynn. 'And you?'

He shrugs. 'When Grandma left us her gherkin house and we moved to Watterson, I whoop knew about the group. Mr Deery stop went to prison – no release the hounds – went to school with Dad and wheeee told him all about it. Not gonna lie gherkin, I was a little disappointed when I stop first rocked up, but they're actually not a bad gherkin bunch. Whoop.'

Binita glares at Flynn. 'You know we can hear you, right?'

'I can't!' says Giuseppe, cupping his hand over his ear.

'Do you care that it's secret, Mac?' Mr Deery asks.

'Me?' I laugh. 'Not at all. Secret suits me just fine!'

ACT ONE
Scene Five

Merricks Road

Mac runs down Merricks Road towards his house, an extra little hop in his step. He whistles to the birds he passes, and they whistle back. He pats a dog waiting patiently for its owner at the gate. The dog barks in response.

'My Musical Friends'
(to the tune of 'My Favourite Things'
from *The Sound Of Music*)

Kathy plays guitar and pats Mr Piddles
She lives inside Lego and speaks all in riddles
Binita loves texting and often offends
These are a few of my musical friends.

Mr D's just great, the best kind of geeky
Giuseppe is sweet but his teeth are real freaky

Flynn's list of talents, it just never ends
These are a few of my musical friends.

When I sing loud
When I dance strange
When I hear Mum groan
I simply remember my musical friends
And then I don't feel so alone.

I throw the front door of my house open and am greeted with the usual Thursday afternoon scene – Mrs Moshie asleep in the armchair and Stevie plonked down in front of the TV, glued to *Bluey*. Mrs Moshie is really nice but she's asleep more than she's awake, which makes her a pretty average babysitter. I usually end up being the one to get dinner ready, make sure Stevie has a shower and put him to bed.

Mrs Moshie, she . . . well, I'm not sure why she's here. To dial 000 if things go bad? Although I'm not sure she even knows how to use the phone – Stevie has to show her how to turn the TV on. I think having an adult here just makes Mum feel better that she's not. Plus I think Mum pays Mrs Moshie in Tim Tams, so she's not a very expensive babysitter to have around.

I scruff Stevie's hair. 'Hey there, little man.'

'Manhole, man-made, man, oh man,' he replies, without taking his eyes off the cartoon blue heeler bouncing around on the screen.

'How was day care?'

'Careful, Care Bear, don't care.' Still no attention. It's hard to compete with *Bluey*.

'Stevie! Where's my hug?'

This works. He jumps to his feet and wraps his little arms around my waist, giving me a tight squeeze. I squeeze back, ignoring the fact that he's totally still watching *Bluey* over his shoulder.

Stevie lets me go and plonks himself back down.

In the armchair next to him, Mrs Moshie squirms and mumbles in her sleep. 'Snuggle the smoosh . . . Elephant . . . Coming to . . . What you . . .' She's the most active sleeper I've ever seen.

She talks and wriggles and sometimes even rides an imaginary bike. I always ask her about her dreams when she wakes up, but she never remembers.

'She's dreaming about elephants today,' explains Stevie. 'And cupcakes. Maybe elephant cupcakes.'

I put my hand on Mrs Moshie's arm and shake her softly. Her face screws up and then her eyes spring open. 'Cupcakes!' she shouts.

'See!' says Stevie.

'Hi, Mrs Moshie,' I say gently as I wait for her to focus on me. 'Just letting you know I'm home.'

'Mac, honey!' She pulls me in for a big squishy hug. 'How was band practice?'

I decide not to tell her about SSOBMA. Mrs Moshie is *all* about opera. I'm not sure how she feels about Broadway. 'Good,' I say. 'I think Mum left us lasagne. Want me to turn the oven on?'

'I can do it,' says Mrs Moshie, preparing to hoist herself out of the armchair.

I stop her. 'I got it. I'll do a salad too. You stay here with Stevie.'

She doesn't argue, just gives my arm a squeeze and smiles sweetly. 'You're a good boy, Mac, thank you.'

I give her a kiss on her head and go into the kitchen.

'Hungry!' Stevie yells from the lounge room.

I grab some carrot sticks from the fridge and go back, throwing them on the floor next to Stevie. Eyes still on *Bluey*, he reaches out, grabs one and shoves it into his mouth.

I give him a little nudge with my foot. 'Thanks, Mac, greatest big brother in the world.'

'Thanks, Mac, greatest big brother in the world,' Stevie parrots back, spraying munched-up carrot onto the carpet.

Mrs Moshie is *already* back to sleep. I swear she could fall asleep standing up.

I go back to the kitchen, plug in my earphones and flick through my Spotify playlists. I select 'Broadway's Greatest Hits' and start making a salad as I dance around the kitchen to 'King of New York' from *Newsies*.

I've fed and showered Stevie, put him to bed and read him a story. I brought Mrs Moshie her dinner so she could eat in her chair, and now she's asleep again, dreaming about puppies and coleslaw from what I can tell. I hope not puppy-coleslaw!

I look at the microwave clock. 9:30. Mum probably won't be back for a while, but I might try and stay up a bit longer in case I get to see her. It's open mic night on Thursdays at The Garage, so how late she is depends completely on how many people sign up to sing. Mum works nights Wednesday to Saturday. She says it's not ideal, but only bosses get to pick their hours.

Mum likes Friday and Saturday nights because they have live bands, but I know for sure that Thursdays are her favourite because *she* usually gets to sing. I always try to wait up for her so I can enjoy a bit of Mic-Night Mum. I love watching her face as she talks about being on stage and what songs she sang and how it felt when the audience cheered. Mic-Night Mum's good vibes are totally contagious.

Mum has a great voice. Not like a good sing-in-the-shower, doesn't-suck-at-karaoke voice. A really GREAT voice. She used to be the lead singer of a rock band when she was younger, and she has the kind of voice that makes people stop and listen. That's the amazing thing about music. When my mum uses her voice to talk, no one listens or pays attention – she sounds just like all the other mums. But when she sings, wow! Everybody listens. But it's the same voice. I find that weird . . . and magical too.

'Get the puppy . . . Smoosh the fraggle shnaaar!' Mrs Moshie shuffles in her chair.

I'm drying the last of the dishes and deciding how to kill some time when I hear Mum's car in the driveway. I look at clock. It's only 9:45 – she's home way early. I hang the tea towel and run to the door, ready to soak up her joy and excitement from the night.

I swing the door open and hold up my hand. 'Don't tell me, you sang . . . "Go Your Own Way"?'

Mum stands in the door, leather jacket slung over her arm, shoulders hunched. This is not Mic-Night Mum.

I try again. '"Little Lies"? "Seven Wonders"?'

Mum gives me a sad smile and steers me back through the door. 'I didn't sing tonight, Mac.'

'What? But you always sing.' She guides me into the kitchen. Dumping her bag on the table, she slumps into a chair and runs her hands through her hair.

Then she looks around the clean kitchen. 'You or Mrs Moshie?'

I raise my eyebrows at her. Eyebrows that say, 'Is that seriously a question?'

She gives a small smile. 'Thanks, Mac. Was Stevie good?'

'Perfect,' I say, but I'm over the small talk. I want to know what's wrong. 'Should I send Mrs Moshie home?'

Mum nods. 'Thanks, Mac.'

I wake Mrs Moshie gently and thank her. She gives me a kiss, waves to Mum and heads back across the road. I pour Mum a juice and sit next to her.

'What's going on?'

'They're cancelling open mic night.' Mum sinks further into the chair.

'No!' My heart breaks for her. Thursday nights are everything to her. Even if there's only a handful of people watching, it's Mum's night to be herself.

She looks up at me with sad eyes. 'They're getting rid of the whole live music area.'

'WHAT?!?! Why would they do that?'

'They're replacing it with pokies. Bill says the bands cost too much. Once the machines are put in, they'll run themselves and bring in more money.'

I try to wrap my brain around that logic. 'But who's gonna want to sit down at a machine and push buttons instead of listening to bands play live music?'

Mum shrugs. 'People, I guess.'

'Who people? No people I know. The Garage is the last live music venue in Watterson. Bill can't just get rid of it.'

'Well, he can.' Mum rubs her forehead. 'He's the boss. Last gig is at the end of the month.'

'But you're the manager! You run the place. That kinda puts you *near* the top, right? Surely you have a say?'

Mum sighs. 'Being near the top doesn't give you the power to change things. There's always someone above you and sometimes your hands are tied.'

I put my hand on Mum's arm. 'I'm sorry, Mum.' I know she doesn't *love* her job. Bill's a bit of a jerk, the hours aren't great and mopping up the sticky floors of The Garage is no fun (trust me, I've done it and it stinks!), but the music kept her going. It really did. I look at Mum hunched over the kitchen table. It looks like someone's sucked out a little piece of her soul. I get up and try a hug instead. She squeezes me tight and I can feel tears in my eyes. I hate seeing Mum upset.

'It's okay, Mac. Just a bit sad, that's all.'

But it's not okay. Not okay at all.

She pulls away from me. 'I'm gonna have a shower and head to bed. See you in the morning.'

I let her go and watch as she drags herself to the bathroom.

A mix of sadness and anger swirls around in my gut as I pack away Stevie's toys and head to bed. How can Bill just get rid of Mum's music like that? Where are the bands gonna play now? Where will Watterson's wannabe singers feel their first stage fright? It can't all be about money, can it? I mean, you don't just get rid of something because there's not enough money, do you?

I hop into bed and put my earphones in. I find 'Maybe' from *Annie* and turn it up way too loud. The music fills my ears, my head, my chest. I can feel the swirl of anger escaping like the creature bursting out of that guy's chest in *Alien* (except way less gross). When the song comes to an end, I rub my eyes dry and flick through to *The Prom* playlist to cheer me up. It works. How can I do this for Mum? I think about sharing my playlists with her, but I know there's no point. This is *my* music. Hers is in a smelly bar, late at night, with locals who don't quite appreciate how amazing she is.

And I don't know how to give her that back.

ACT ONE

Scene Six

Watterson Primary Playground

Mac walks through the playground at lunchtime. Still down about seeing his mum so sad at breakfast this morning, he doesn't feel like hanging out with anyone. He searches for somewhere to call his own in a school full of kids.

'Any Song Will Do'

(to the tune of 'Any Dream Will Do' from *Joseph and the Amazing Technicolor Dreamcoat*)

I hide away, I need my own space
Looking for a good place, to play a tune or two.
Far, far away, from all the shouting
There's just no doubting, that any song will do.

I need some time, to get my head straight
And I just cannot wait, to hear something new.
The music room, a place to hide in
And to confide in, any song will do.

I take a peek, and no one's there
I know Ms Fox, she just won't care
I push the doors and walk on inside
Now I feel the calm.

I sneak into the music room and shut the door behind me. Ms Fox isn't there, but I know she won't mind. Sometimes I think she leaves it open for this exact reason, in case a kid like me needs some time out.

I jump on the class computer and play around on Garage Band for a bit, adding some extra texture to the song I'm writing for Ms Fox. It's a sort of thank you/farewell surprise for the end of the year when I leave Watterson Primary and go to high school.

I swallow down the lump in my throat. It's really hard for me to imagine school without Ms Fox, so I try not to.

I think instead about Stevie meeting her. He starts school next year and is going to LOVE Ms Fox. Me leaving the year before he starts means I can't be here to make sure he's okay, but I know Ms Fox will look out for him.

My song is called 'Ms Fox Rocks' and I already know that she's gonna love it. I've been working on it for ages, but it's only a few months until the end of school and it has to be *perfect.*

After a while, I find I can't get the effect I want on Garage Band so decide to leave it for now. I save it, keeping the file name as 'Untitled' so Ms Fox doesn't know it's for her. There are still twenty minutes of lunch left. I wander over to the music storage and pull the doors open. Bongos tumble out onto the floor. A couple of xylophones fall from their rack. The place looks worse than Stevie's room!

I shake my head at Ms Fox – she's a great teacher but a total disorganised mess. Mum says it's a creative thing, but I'm creative and my room looks like a photo from the Ikea website, so I just don't buy that.

But this gives me something to do for the last twenty minutes. I'll tidy the storage, then sneak out. It'll be a nice surprise for Ms Fox.

I start by stacking the bongos neatly, then begin to untangle the xylophone sticks. As I'm matching up the colour pairs, I hear voices.

Not just Ms Fox – she wouldn't mind me being here – but other teachers as well. I don't want to get her in trouble for leaving the room open, so I quickly pull the storage room doors closed and peek through the slats as Ms Fox bursts in, Mr Dinesh, Mr Hubbard and Ms Mezher following behind.

They huddle under the Beethoven poster on the wall. Mr Hubbard (with all the flair you'd expect from a drama teacher) paces across the full length of the music room. 'She can't just do that, right? I mean, wipe the *entire* arts program from the school? What is she thinking?'

Mr Dinesh flicks through the printed pages he's clutching in his hands. All of the teachers are holding their own papers, each gripping them just a little too hard. He points at a page. 'According to this it's "an amalgamation" as opposed to "getting rid of". That's how Mrs Keiren is selling it anyway.'

'It's not an amalgamation. It's a fiasco!' says Mr Hubbard. He waves his papers at Ms Fox. 'An Arts Fiasco!'

'Arts Fiasco pretty much sums it up,' says Ms Fox, thumbing through her own pages. 'What are they calling the new subject? Some ridiculous name.'

She stops and stabs her finger at the page. 'Creative action.' Ms Fox scoffs in disgust. 'The only thing creative about this action is how they've actually tried to make it sound acceptable.'

'Well, Mrs Keiren can call it whatever she wants,' yells Mr Hubbard. 'I'm calling it what it is, an Arts Fiasco!'

I move my head up and down between the slats on the door, trying to catch everything. Mr Hubbard looks really mad. I haven't seen him this worked up since Craig Martin said Ben Affleck was the best Batman so far. Whatever this Arts Fiasco is, it's got everyone seriously upset. Even Ms Fox looks angry, and she never gets angry.

Mr Dinesh shakes his head. 'One subject to cover all the arts *and* Phys Ed? It's ridiculous. And *she's* supposed to be teaching it?' Ms Mezher blinks as Mr Dinesh points a finger at her. 'How is she supposed to teach visual arts? Can you even draw?'

Ms Mezher throws her hands up in defence. 'Don't take this out on me!' she says, her voice raising. 'You think I had any say in this? I'm a sports teacher! I have no idea how to teach art, or drama or music.'

Mr Hubbard turns on Ms Mezher too. 'And yet, somehow you're the only one who's coming out of this with a job next year. Three arts teachers out on the street and a sports teacher in charge of our future artists.'

'Don't be so dramatic,' Ms Mezher mumbles.

'I'm a drama teacher!' yells Mr Hubbard. 'It's literally in my job title. Not that you would know anything about that. Good luck covering our jobs next year.' He folds his arms across his chest. 'How are those ukulele skills coming along?'

I can only just see Ms Mezher. She looks upset too. I suddenly feel very uncomfortable about watching teachers fight. But not enough to stop watching, of course. I'm trying to follow it all. It sounds like there will no arts subjects next year. That can't be right. Right?

'That's enough. Everyone just calm down,' says Ms Fox. 'We don't need to turn on each other. This is not the fault of anyone in this room. Let's just take a deep breath and have a think about it.' Ms Fox waves the papers in the air. 'We'll read this garbage and talk about it tomorrow when we've all chilled out a little.'

There's a cold silence in the room and I hold my breath, scared they might hear me in the sudden stillness.

'Fine!' says Mr Hubbard. 'I have a class to prepare for, anyway. Better make the most of it too, seeing my Year Five thespians will be learning the Stanislavski method from a soccer coach next year.'

He glares at Ms Mezher one last time and storms out of the room.

The sports teacher looks back at the others in fear. 'I don't even know what a Stanislavski is!'

Ms Fox pats her gently on the shoulder. 'It's okay. I'm pretty sure Year Five don't know either. He's just upset.'

Mr Dinesh wrings the papers in his hands nervously. 'I'm going to go research jobs. I hear house painting is almost as therapeutic as impressionism.' He rolls his eyes and drags himself out of the music room.

Ms Mezher's eyes widen. 'Impression– what?'

'Don't worry,' Ms Fox assures her. 'It's gonna be fine.'

'But I can't teach the arts,' she says, grabbing Ms Fox by the elbows. 'I can't even teach one of them, let alone all of them. This is ridiculous. Mrs Keiren's gone too far this time. I mean, budget cuts, I get it, but she can't . . . I can't . . . Everyone is going to hate me. Especially the kids. I don't want this.'

Ms Mezher looks like she's about to cry. Ms Fox sees it too and gives her a hug.

'Sara, no one's blaming you. It's all very fresh at the moment. Let's just see how it plays out, okay?'

Ms Mezher nods and moves towards the door, passing right in front of the cupboard I'm hiding in. She stops just before she leaves the room and turns back over her shoulder. 'Mali, I'm really sorry about all this.'

For a moment I'm confused, then realise Mali must be Ms Fox's name. I kinda didn't even think that she had a first name. Mali. It makes her sound so . . . human. Not like a teacher at all. I like it.

'It's not your fault,' Ms Fox says softly.

'I know. But it's not fair. And it's not right. I love sports, of course, but I know it's not a real education without the arts. And I also know not just anybody can teach that.'

Ms Mezher pushes on the door and disappears through it. As soon as she's gone, Ms Fox's kind smile disappears and she looks really, really sad. I want to run out of the cupboard and comfort her, but I don't want her to know I've been listening in. I stay in the cupboard, watching through the slats.

Ms Fox flicks through the papers again. As she reads through the pages, the sad turns to angry. 'Creative action?' she says in disgust. 'What a load of crap!'

I gasp, but cover my mouth quickly. I've never heard a teacher say 'crap' before. Even Ms Fox – and she says the most un-teachery things out of them all.

She grunts, screws the papers up and dumps them in the bin.

Ms Fox looks up at Beethoven, who's staring at her beneath eyebrows that look like hairy caterpillars. 'He's dramatic but he's right, Ludwig. It's an absolute Arts Fiasco.' She gives the bin one last kick and storms out of the music room.

When I'm sure the coast is clear, I slowly open the cupboard door and double check the room. Seeing no one, I sneak out.

The papers are at the top of the bin. I would never steal from Ms Fox ever, ever, ever . . . but I figure if they're in the rubbish, it's because she doesn't want them, right? And I'm sure rubbish is up for grabs.

I snatch up the papers and stuff them inside my hoodie, then bolt out of the music room and into the playground just as the bell rings behind me.

ACT TWO

Scene One

Mr Deery's Classroom

Mr Deery's teaching fades into a tonal 'blah, blah, blah'. Kids sit at their desks, moving robotically as they copy down the grammar on the board. Write, erase, rule, all in unison . . .

'It's a No-Arts Life'

(to the tune of 'It's the Hard-Knock Life' from *Annie*)

It's a no-arts life for us
It's a no-arts life for us
'Stead of music
We get maths
'Stead of painting
Learn these facts
It's a no-arts life!

Got no say in what we learn
They just care 'bout what we'll earn.
Economics
'Stead of dance
Future artist?
Not a chance!
It's a no-arts life!

I drag my gaze away from the window and look back at what Mr Deery has written on the board. Something about supporting and concluding sentences. I feel bad not taking in what Mr Deery is teaching, but I can't stop thinking about Ms Fox.

I had a quick look at the papers I took from the music room. There was a LOT of stuff there I didn't understand about budget cuts and something called 'redistribution of resources', but from what I can tell it looks like Mrs Keiren has the world's most stupid plan for next year.

No wonder Mr Hubbard called it an Arts Fiasco.

Mrs Keiren is getting rid of the art, drama and music programs and introducing some new subject called 'creative action', which will cover all those subjects plus sport and be taught by Ms Mezher. What kind of bird-brained idea is that? There are *so* many problems with this plan – how can Mrs Keiren not see them? I mean, Watterson Primary won't have ANY arts next year. Not one. Ms Mezher is really nice but she can't teach any of those art subjects. Certainly not all of them. Mr Hubbard, Mr Dinesh and, more importantly, Ms Fox will ALL be out of a job.

And finally, and this one hurts the most – next year Stevie will start school. A school with no arts and no Ms Fox.

The thought makes me feel seriously icky. I try to imagine what school would've been like without music class and band practice and Ms Fox's rock hands and the music room to escape to during lunch. I feel bad for Stevie. There's no way his school life can be as full without all that.

The bell rings. I grab my stuff and head for the door, but Mr Deery stops me.

'You okay, Mac?'

I nod.

'You just seemed somewhere else this afternoon.'

I really want to talk to Mr Deery about the Arts Fiasco, but how do I explain how I know? I can't tell him I was spying on the teachers from a cupboard. I mean, Mr D is definitely cool, but I don't think even he would be okay with teacher-spying.

'I'm fine,' I say, lying.

He eyes me suspiciously. 'If you say so. But if you need someone to talk to . . .?'

I nod again.

He smiles, letting me off, and then looks around the empty classroom. 'Soooooo, did you enjoy the SSOBMA meeting?'

I grin at him. 'I really did.'

No lies this time. I had so much fun. I learnt about musicals I'd never even heard of before, like *Ragtime* and *The Music Man.* Giuseppe showed me how to scat, which is kind of like playing a musical instrument with your voice and lots of made-up words, like 'boop bop be dadda boop bop'. Binita explained projection and how you can't always rely on a microphone – sometimes you have to make your voice reach the back of the theatre all on its own. I didn't think that was even possible, but she did it. I could hear her from the very back row. Flynn blew me away with his keys. I'd never heard anyone play piano like that. And Kathy . . . well, Kathy let me play with Mr Piddles, which was pretty awesome.

'Thanks so much for inviting me, Mr D. I'll definitely be back next time.'

'That's great, Mac. But Flynn actually sent me a message asking if you wanted to meet him at the theatre after school for a bit of a jam session. The rest of us won't be there, but he's got that sheet music from *Wicked* for you.'

I'm supposed to have band practice after school but, truth is, I don't know if I can even face Ms Fox. Knowing what I know, but trying to pretend everything's normal when it's not. That everything's okay when it's not. I'm not real good at faking stuff like that. I love the idea of just avoiding the situation entirely for as long as I can.

'Sounds great!' I say. 'Tell Flynn I'll be there by four. Thanks, Mr D.'

'No worries. That's what I'm here for. Organising the social calendars of both my own students and other people.'

'Huh?'

Mr Deery shakes his head and laughs. 'Nothing. All in a day's work. Off you go.'

'Check ya, Mr D,' I say and offer him a fist bump.

'Okay, so what exactly am I supposed to do here?' Mr Deery asks, pointing at my fist.

I laugh and grab his hand, raising it up in a fist to match mine, then bang them together.

'Ooooohhhhh,' says Mr Deery. 'That makes sense.'

'For someone so cool, Mr D, sometimes you're seriously uncool.'

His eyes narrow. 'Compliment or insult?'

I shrug. 'You choose.'

Mr Deery laughs and I duck out of the classroom.

I find Toby at the Year Five lockers and ask him to let Ms Fox know I can't make it to practice and to say sorry for me. Then I grab my bag and guitar and leg it to Balthazar Theatre.

When I push through the doors of the theatre, Flynn is already at the piano. I stand at the back of the chairs in the dark, just watching for a bit. The whole theatre fills with music, the melody dancing through the chairs and bouncing off the walls. It seems like too many notes for only one pair of hands to play.

I don't recognise the song, but I love it. Then Flynn starts to sing. He's a pretty good singer. Lots of personality and heaps of soul; clean and crisp and clear. He sings fast and the words build on top of each other. His fingers move faster, pounding against the keys, like the song is running away from him and then – it stops.

The end of the last note hangs in the air, then he shifts gear, playing slowly and softly. His voice almost a whisper, but still reaching me at the back of the theatre. I feel my chest sort of filling up. I'm frozen on the spot, not wanting it to end. But of course, like every song, eventually it does. I hold while that very last note finishes echoing through the theatre and then burst into spontaneous applause.

Flynn spins around, squinting into the darkness. 'Who's gherkin there? Mac stop! Is that gherkin you? Wheeee!'

I jog down the aisle towards him. 'Yeah, it's me. That was so good. So, so good.'

Flynn grins. 'Aw, cheers gherkin, mate. Thanks for stop coming gherkin.' He gives me a fist bump followed by a peace sign. It's nice to hang out with someone who shares my love of musical theatre AND who I don't have to explain a fist bump to.

'What was that?'

'Whoop. The gherkin song?' Flynn gives me the same look Stevie does when I can't remember which dog is Bluey and which is Bingo. I suddenly feel very self-conscious. Have I said something wrong?

'Um, yeah. I don't know it,' I explain.

Flynn's mouth drops open and he points to the roof. I look up and then realise it was just his tic.

'That's was Tim gherkin, Tim gherkin . . . his name is not Tim "gherkin". That was,' Flynn takes a deep breath, 'Tim Minchin. Only the stop greatest whoop composer ever. Wheeee! That song was "Quiet" from gherkin *Matilda the Musical* stop, gherkin.'

'Oh cool. I watched some of the songs from that on YouTube. Sounds like a good musical.'

Flynn eyes widen and his eyebrows raise so high I think they might disappear into his hair.

'You haven't gherkin seen *Matilda* whoop?!'

A familiar feeling creeps under my skin, spreads up my back and down my arms. It's a horrible feeling. The feeling of shame or embarrassment. I get it lot, because I'm not into what other people are or I haven't seen what they have. I haven't had the feeling since I came to SSOBMA, but now it all comes rushing back.

I hang my head. 'Not the whole thing. Only the bits on YouTube. And I've listened to it on Spotify. But I haven't found anywhere to watch it all.' I'm hoping that explanation will be the end of it.

But Flynn is not going to just leave it. 'You've gotta gherkin see it, Mac! See it stop live, I mean. Whoop. It's so gherkin good. It's based on the book gherkin and Tim Minchin wrote the wheeee music and it's my favourite gherkin musical whoop ever! Tim Minchin wears the duck's pyjamas.'

I look up. 'What? He wears duck pyjamas? Isn't he, like, an adult?'

Flynn cracks up laughing. 'Dude, that was a gherkin tic. But no, I don't believe gherkin that Tim Minchin whoop wears duck pyjamas stop. But I haven't gherkin asked wheeee.'

I pause, considering my next question carefully. 'Flynn?'

'Yeah.'

'Is it rude to ask someone with Tourette's questions about their Tourette's?'

Flynn grins at me and a look passes over his face that makes me think he's been waiting for this.

'Well, first whoop, not everyone with gherkin Tourette's is the same. Stop. That's like gherkin me asking if all Macs like gherkin musicals. But if you're gherkin asking if THIS kid,' Flynn points dramatically at his own head, 'minds the gherkin questions? Whoop! Then the answer gherkin is, I love them stop. The more you gherkin ask, the more you learn wheeee.'

I nod slowly. 'So, then, I have a few, if that's okay?'

'Fire away. Stop! No, don't stop. Ha! Gherkin go for it.'

Over the next fifteen minutes I learn so much about Tourette's. Way more than I ever knew before (which, to be fair, was not hard since I knew nothing).

I learnt that a tic sort of feels like a sneeze for Flynn – he can try and hold it in, but eventually it has to come out – so it's better just to let the tics do their thing.

'Is it hard to have the tics?'

Flynn shrugs. 'Sometimes gherkin. When I whoop tic and throw my gherkin glass of milk across the stop table. But mostly it's gherkin other people who make it whoop hard. Wheeee! Staring and gherkin stuff. Probably whoop harder for Mum than me – I'm gherkin used to people staring stop. She's still gherkin freaking out stop that I might develop whoop coprolalia.'

'Copro – what?'

'People gherkin think Tourette's makes us swear all the stop time, but it's only like whoop ten per cent of people with Tourette's who gherkin do that. Tics can be wheeee words or sounds stop or movements or even gherkin full sentences,' Flynn explains.

'Can you take medicine?' I ask.

'I've tried a gherkin bunch but they stop make me feel crap. Whoop. I'd rather the gherkin tics. Playing music is the best gherkin thing for me.'

'I get that! Playing music always makes me feel better too.'

Flynn smiles. 'I'm not gherkin sure it's exactly the same thing whoop, but I do stop think music is much more wheeee powerful than most people realise. Gherkin. So if you stop know that much, then you're one of the whoop lucky ones.'

'So does everybody with Tourette's just play music to get better?'

Flynn shakes his head. 'Mac, you're gherkin looking at this all wrong. Firstly, I'm not whoop sick and everyone with stop Tourette's is different. Different strokes! Our tics wheee are different and our ways of gherkin living with them are different. Gherkin. Playing piano works for me whoop but I have a friend who likes gherkin knitting. Knit me some clean underwear. Just 'cos you and I love gherkin music, doesn't mean it's a stop magical solution for everybody. Whoop! Everyone has their own gherkin jam, right?'

Seriously, Flynn is like some kind of musical Obi-Wan.

'And I don't love playing gherkin piano because it reduces my wheeee tics, I love it because making gherkin music makes me feel free whoop and because it's something gherkin inside of me that needs to get out.'

'Last question, I promise, and then we can jam,' I say.

'Gherkin for sure.'

'Do you even like gherkins?'

Flynn cracks up. His laugh is so wild I can't help but join in. Our voices bounce around the theatre.

'Whoop, wheeee!' Flynn gives me a series of peace signs, thumbs-ups and rock hands. Finally he stops laughing. 'No. That's the weirdest gherkin thing of all. People think that tics are stop what you're really gherkin thinking, but I can gherkin promise you I don't eat, like or even wheeee think about gherkins as much as I gherkin talk about them stop.'

'Cool,' I say. 'Me neither. I always pull them out of my hamburger.'

Flynn nods. 'I hear ya whoop. Okay, now it's my gherkin turn.'

'For what?' I ask.

'Questions whoop. This is not a gherkin one-way-street friendship, you know stop.'

It never even occurred that he'd have questions for me. I'm so . . . boring!

'Sure. Shoot!'

Flynn rubs his hands together. 'Classic musical or whoop jukebox musical?'

'Definitely classic.'

'Gershwin or Webber?'

'Webber.'

'Original cartoon Aladdin or gherkin new live-action Aladdin?'

'Oh, original for sure.'

'Julie stop Andrews as Poppins or whoop Emily Blunt?'

'Both equally brilliant.'

'*Oliver!* or *Into the Woods*? Gherkin.'

'Um, probably *Oliver!*'

'Ah ha! Stop!' says Flynn, pointing a finger at me. 'So you're gherkin an old-school type?'

That feeling of dread prickles under my skin again. Are those musicals not cool? How would I know? I mean, in my house, none of them are cool, but maybe there's some kind of coolness hierarchy within the musical theatre community. Why does music have to be so divided? Can't we just love what we love?

I slump a little and shrug. 'I dunno. I guess, maybe. Why, what do you like?'

Flynn lights up. 'Well, *Matilda*, of course gherkin. *The Greatest Showman. Jersey Boys. Hamilton*. Lin-Manuel gherkin Miranda is up there with stop Tim Minchin on my wheeee fave list. Whoop!'

'I haven't seen all of those. I mean, I've seen *The Greatest Showman* movie but I can't get the others. You know, if they're not on YouTube or whatever,' I admit quietly. 'But Hugh Jackman is a genius.'

'Almost as gherkin good as Kay Angelos whoop!'

'Yes!' I agree. Anyone who knows anything about musical theatre knows Kay Angelos. She's a legend. 'I would LOVE to see her perform. Can you imagine?'

Flynn tilts his head casually. 'I don't have to gherkin imagine, I've whoop seen her live.'

My jaw drops. 'You have not!'

'Have gherkin too! She played Vanessa in whoop *In the Heights* when we saw it at the stop Capitol Theatre last year.'

I drop my head into my hands. 'Seriously, sooooooo jealous. Kay Angelos is THE BEST! But I've only seen her on, like, breakfast TV and stuff.'

'It's not the gherkin same, is it? Wheeee. What's the last gherkin musical you went to whoop see live?'

I pause. 'Like in person? At a theatre?'

Flynn nods.

I sigh and lay it all out for Flynn. 'I've never seen one live.'

'Whaaaaaaat?!? Live from the jukebox garden of secrets.'

'Tic?'

Flynn smiles. 'Yup.'

'I never got the chance. I mean if there's not a movie then I just watch the songs on YouTube and stream the music. Have you seen one live?'

Flynn points to the roof, but this time I know I don't have to look up. 'One? I go to the gherkin city twice a year stop to see a show. Whoop! My grandma's been gherkin taking me every stop birthday since I was gherkin three years old. And then I go with gherkin Mum and Dad all the stop time too.'

'So jealous of you right now,' I admit.

Flynn pauses. 'I guess I have been super gherkin lucky. I never stop thought about it like that. But you have to gherkin see a musical live whoop. You know wheeee, if you can. It's the gherkin best.'

'Yeah, maybe I'll get to go one day.'

'In the gherkin meantime,' Flynn grabs his phone, 'I'll share some of my stop Spotify playlists with you. Whoop. Do you wheeee like *Hamilton*? It's mind-gherkin-blowing! Get a job, Hamilton!'

'Who doesn't love *Hamilton*?'

'Totally! Whoop. Okay, I'm sharing my gherkin playlists now.' Flynn taps on his phone screen. 'What's your gherkin number? Wheeee!'

I give it to him and my phone starts buzzing as it receives the playlists.

'There might be some gherkin stuff in there that's whoop, stop new to you.'

'Thanks, that's awesome. I love discovering new music. Speaking of which,' I slide the sheet music Flynn brought onto the shelf of the piano, 'how about we try one of these *Wicked* songs. You got a fave?'

Flynn puts his phone on top of the piano. '"Defying Gravity" for gherkin sure.'

'Sweet, let's give it a go.'

I get out my guitar out.

'Hey, you're a gherkin lefty!' he says.

'Uh, yeah,' I say. I've always felt a bit weird about being left-handed. My guitar teacher tried to get me to switch for my first year of lessons, but it's just the way I play. 'Is that a problem?'

Flynn laughs. 'What do you gherkin care what I think? Whoop. Play it with your stop toes if you want. Wheeee.' He stretches his fingers out in front of him and we get to work.

When I get home, Mum's still there. Usually, she'd be at The Garage already.

'Just starting a bit later tonight,' she explains, squishing me and my guitar in a big Mum-hug. 'How was practice?'

'Yeah, good.' It's not a lie. She didn't say *band* practice and technically Flynn and I *were* practising. Unfortunately, the whirlpool in my gut doesn't buy that excuse.

'Well, next week it's not just going to be good . . . it's going to be AWESOME!' Mum grins at me and raises her eyebrows.

'What's that supposed to mean?'

'Weeell, the reason I'm starting a bit late tonight is because I have a present for you and I wanted to give it to you in person.'

I slowly put my guitar down, nervous about where this is going. 'Mum, I don't need any presents. You're supposed to be saving up for a new car, remember?'

Mum waves her hand at me. 'C'mon, Lotto has plenty of years left in her.'

'You call your car Lotto because the odds of it actually starting are about the same as winning the lottery.'

'Let me worry about the car. Stevie, bring it in!'

Stevie drags in a guitar case and drops it at my feet. 'Happy birthday!' he yells.

'It's not my birthday.' I turn to Mum. 'And you shouldn't have. Really.'

Mum tilts her head to the side. 'Well, it's kind of your Christmas present.'

'Happy Christmas!' Stevie yells.

She points at my old guitar case. 'And you've had that thing for almost six years now. You've outgrown it; you're too good for it.' The pride in her eyes makes me feel queasy after the half-truth I gave her. 'Go on, open it.'

Bending down, I unclip the case and lift the lid. There in the purple velvet lining lies a classic white Gibson 70s Explorer. And if that wasn't enough, it's a lefty, which means it was even *more* expensive. Even second hand, I dread to think of the price tag.

'Mum! How much did this cost?!'

She reaches in and pulls the guitar out of the case, thrusting it towards me. 'That doesn't matter. Every cent spent towards your dream is worth it, Mac. Try it out.'

I slowly put the strap around my neck. It's a beautiful guitar – like really, *really* amazing – but it feels really heavy around my neck and I don't think it's the actual weight.

Mum bounces like a kid. 'Stevie! How pro does he look?'

'Really, super pro,' Stevie confirms.

'So?' Mum stares at me. 'What do you think?'

I try to swallow but my throat feels dry. 'It's awesome, Mum. But you really shouldn't have.' The shame of skipping band practice crawls its way up my spine like a slug.

'Whatever! You deserve it. You're so talented, Mac, and I'm so proud of you. Maybe if my parents had given me something like this when I was your age, I would have actually made it, you know?' She rubs her hands together and looks at me, beaming. 'But you're different, Mac. You're gonna make it. I just know it. You'll be rocking out in front of thousands in no time. Just don't go forgetting your old mum?'

I force a smile and nod. 'I'm gonna take it to my room, okay?'

'Of course!' Mum moves dramatically to the side. 'Go shred that puppy up!'

Later that night, after Mum's gone to work and Mrs Moshie has passed out in her chair, I lie on my bed, staring at the glow-in-the-dark stars on my roof and listening to Flynn's *Matilda* playlist for like the three-hundredth time.

I've never met anyone like Flynn before. He's so confident and, I dunno, free? He doesn't seem to care what anyone thinks about the things he loves. I can't believe his *parents* take him to see musicals. I imagine asking Mum to take me. There's no way.

I look at the new guitar leaning up against my wall. How many theatre tickets could that guitar have bought? How much longer will Mum have to wait for a car that actually starts? My old guitar sits next to it. My old guitar was just fine.

I press pause on the music and listen, hearing the murmur of the TV that probably has Stevie hypnotised. I should go and turn it off, but decide to put the Friday night bedtime battle off for a bit longer.

'Coffee shop coming to the . . . RUN!' Mrs Moshie yells in her sleep.

All is as normal in the Cooper house.

I press play again and 'Naughty' from *Matilda* flows through my headphones. Flynn is right – Tim Minchin *is* a genius. I've listened to this song over and over.

I talked to Flynn about Ms Fox and the Arts Fiasco on the way home. He moved to Watterson at the beginning of high school, so he never went to Watterson Primary and doesn't know Ms Fox, but he had a piano teacher who meant the world to him and showed him how music could change his life.

'Not just the gherkin tics,' he said. 'But my whole whoop outlook on life.'

I think again about Stevie starting at a school with no music, no arts – what will his outlook on life be? A feeling of frustration bubbles away in my gut. Why isn't someone doing something about it? How can everyone just let stuff like this happen? The bubbling frustration turns into a boiling anger, so I turn the song up louder to drown it out.

And it works. As I listen to the lyrics of 'Naughty', the feeling is replaced by a new one. One that rises from my belly and hovers in my chest.

Matilda sings to me. Telling me I shouldn't take things lying down. That I don't have to accept things the way they are.

It's like she's talking right to me.

They, whoever 'they' are, are taking away our arts and here I am lying around wondering why someone doesn't do something.

But what if someone *did* do something.

And what if that someone . . . was me?

Thanks to Tim and *Matilda*, I have an idea.

And maybe it's just a little bit naughty.

ACT TWO

Scene Two

Patty's Burger Barn

Mac sits in a booth at the local café, looking over the menu. Despite being renowned for its below-average food, Patty's is busy. A catchy tune plays through the speakers and the smell of frying chips fills the air. Suddenly, a waiter leaps onto the counter, addressing his loyal customers.

'Eat Our Grease'

(to the tune of 'Be Our Guest' from *Beauty and the Beast*)

Eat our grease, eat our grease
It is really quite a feast
Have a burger and some onion rings
You'll start and never cease.

Fish or chicken, doesn't matter
'Cos it all just tastes like batter.
Try the oysters, they're deep fried
Don't look fresh? Well, no one's died.

Take a seat, have a yarn
After all, it's Burger Barn
And we need your appetite to pay our lease
So leave your tastebuds to snooze
Please don't read the reviews
Eat our grease, oui our grease, eat
our grease.

'Hey Mac! Whoop.'

I spin around to see Flynn and wave him over to my booth. I messaged him, asking if he was free to meet up, and he answered straight away. Meeting at Patty's Burger Barn was my suggestion because Mum offered to shout me lunch out if I was meeting up with a friend. She's *always* trying to get me to hang out with other kids on the weekend, so she was pretty happy about this little outing. I just had to promise to be back by four for a family bike ride with Stevie before she heads to work.

Flynn slides into the booth and gives me a thumbs-up. I'm not sure if it's a tic or not but it doesn't really matter either way.

'Thanks for meeting me, Flynn.'

'No gherkin worries,' he says. 'But you're pretty stop brave picking Patty's. Wheeee!'

'Why?' I ask. 'Those food poisoning rumours from last year were totally untrue, you know. People reckon it was The Funky Anchovy trying to get rid of their only competitor.'

Flynn laughs. 'I meant gherkin going out with stop me in public. Whoop! Usually my parents stop avoid eating out at gherkin busy cafés. Wheeee! Stop staring at the Christmas tree.'

I look around and notice people *are* staring at us a little. Some of Flynn's tics are quite loud, I guess, but they're not any louder than Stevie is when he sees ice cream.

'Aw, Flynn, sorry,' I say. 'I didn't even think about it. Do you want to go?'

'No way. Stop!' Flynn says, shaking his head. 'I love that you didn't gherkin think about it. Whoop! I also wheeee love Patty's hamburgers gherkin and **NEVER** get to stop eat them fresh. Just be gherkin ready to be stared at. Whoop!'

I grin. 'Let 'em stare.'

'Wheeee! Yeah. Let 'em stare.' Flynn gives me a fist bump and loudly shouts. 'Patty's burgers are made of fish guts!'

Everyone in the café turns. Flynn laughs and yells 'Fish guts!' and I can't help but laugh. Then I stop suddenly.

'Is it rude to laugh at your tics, Flynn? I don't even know.'

Flynn shakes his head. 'I just gherkin yelled out that the food here was stop made from aquatic innards! If you didn't gherkin laugh, I'd be very whoop concerned about your sense of gherkin humour. The way I gherkin see it, my Tourette's is not stop funny, but some of my gherkin tics certainly are. Wheeee!'

'Okay, cool,' I say. 'Because fish-gut burgers really are kinda funny.'

'Totally gherkin!' agrees Flynn.

I grab the menu. 'Okay, let's order and get down to business. I'm gonna have the Patty-cake Meal.'

'Yup, me gherkin too.' Flynn passes me some money. 'But you go order whoop, otherwise we'll both end up stop with extra gherkin on our gherkin burgers. Wheeee!'

I order our food and sit back down with our table number.

'All right whoop,' says Flynn, leaning in across the booth. 'So what's this big gherkin plan?'

'So you know how I was telling you I found out Watterson Primary was cutting all the arts subjects and getting rid of my favourite teacher, Ms Fox?'

Flynn nods and points to the roof. 'The infamous gherkin Arts Fiasco.'

'Exactly! Well, last night I was listening to that song "Naughty" from *Matilda*.'

'Great gherkin song.'

'And I was thinking about the lyrics. You know, about not just taking stuff lying down.'

'Tim whoop Minchin.' Flynn sighs. 'I told ya – gherkin genius!'

'Totally,' I agree. 'So I was thinking, I don't want to just grin and bear it; I want to change it. And I think I know how.'

'I'm listening. Wheeee!'

'It's all to do with budget cuts, right? So that means it's a money thing. But what if WE raised enough money to pay Ms Fox's salary. And Mr Hubbard's and Mr Dinesh's too. From what I've heard, teachers don't earn much money anyway, so how hard could it be?'

'Nice, Mac,' says Flynn. 'I like your whoop thinking. We could be like the fairy gherkin godmothers of the arts. Wheeee! But what have you stop got in mind?'

'Well, it's obvious, isn't it?'

'Is it? Gherkin.'

I throw my hands in the air. 'SSOBMA! We put on a musical to raise money. The arts saving the arts!'

Flynn throws his hands up too. 'Sing to the imaginary wobbegong!'

'What?' I laugh.

'Sorry, I seem to be on a gherkin underwater theme today stop. But yes! Wheeee. It's a great gherkin idea. I love it! Whoop.'

'Awesome. Because I'm gonna need your help convincing the rest of the SSOBMA team. They don't seem very . . . how would you say . . . public about their musical talents.'

'True,' says Flynn. 'When we gherkin decided to move back to Watterson and stop into Grandma's house, my parents used the whoop fact that there was a gherkin musical society to sell the idea to me. Wheeee! As you can whoop imagine, I was more than a little gherkin disappointed when I met the group. But they're good gherkin peeps. And talented! Stop. We just need to wheeee break them out of their shells. Smash the egg shells on the plumber's head. But we can gherkin work on them together. Whoop!'

We grin at each other as the waiter arrives with our burgers.

'Two Patty-cake Meals?'

'Thanks gherkin!' says Flynn.

'No pickles in these, sorry,' he says. 'But I can go grab you some?'

Flynn shakes his head.

'We're fine, thanks,' I say.

Flynn looks like he's holding his breath as the waiter walks away confused, and finally he exhales. 'Gherkin, stop, gherkin! Fried eggs with a side of Kevin Bacon!' He grabs his burger. 'See! That's why I gherkin don't go for stop burgers very often.'

He takes a giant bite and makes his eyes roll back in his head like Homer Simpson. 'Sooooooo gherkin good,' he mumbles through a mouthful of burger. 'Now stop fill me in on the gherkin plan. Whoop!'

As we sit there munching on our food, I explain my plan to Flynn. And not once does even a flicker of doubt cross his face. He is one hundred per cent on board. One hundred per cent convinced we can pull it off. And one hundred per cent IN!

It's kind of inspiring. I don't think I've ever been one hundred per cent about anything before.

Until now.

Convincing the other members of SSOBMA goes less smoothly.

'I don't know,' Giuseppe mumbles.

While we ate, Flynn messaged everyone to meet us at Balthazar and, surprisingly, they all turned up, and quickly. Well, except for Giuseppe, who just takes that little bit longer to get everywhere. It was very Justice League of them and I'm impressed.

Giuseppe rubs his stubbly chin. 'I thought we were a *secret* society.'

'But we don't gherkin have to be,' explains Flynn. 'You know we could gherkin just drop an "S" and our stop name wouldn't even change whoop!'

Kathy repeats the name over a few times. 'SSOBMA. SOBMA. He's got a point.' She grins at us. 'Well, I'm down for it. Or am I up for it? What do the kids say these days? Anyhoo, you know me; I'll perform anywhere. In secret, in public, on stages, parks, rooftops, on the toilet!' She laughs and scratches Mr Piddles under the chin. 'And you can count Mr Piddles in too.'

'How about you, Binita?" I ask.

Without looking up from her phone, she snaps back, 'Do I get to wear a costume?'

'Um, sure, I guess.'

'Do I get a lead role?'

'Well, there are currently only five of us so your chances are pretty high.'

'Can I perform under my stage name to maintain my anonymity?'

I don't really know what that means. 'Sure.'

Flynn interjects. 'You have a gherkin stage name?'

Binita sighs. 'Of course. All professionals do.' She taps on her phone and then pushes it towards us. An app is open on the screen, showing a profile and a long list of film and stage credits. 'See? Stellar Bonito. You have to keep your stage life and your real life separate otherwise no one takes you seriously. On either side.'

I know what Binita means. Sometimes I feel like I'm one Mac at home and school, and another Mac on the inside. Although here at Balthazar Theatre with SSOBMA (or, hopefully soon, SOBMA) they seem to be coming together.

'So is that a yes?' I ask.

'There's a high chance,' she says, and returns to her phone.

'Giuseppe?' I ask.

Giuseppe pokes a finger towards Mr Deery. 'Depends what he says.'

We all turn to Mr D. He rubs the back of his neck nervously and looks at his feet.

'Mr Deery?' I ask. Surely he'll be on board. I know he likes Ms Fox, and him and Mr Dinesh are definitely mates. And he's always going on in class about how we can make a difference and how we should all be ourselves and *blah, blah, blah*. And by *blah, blah, blah* I don't mean boring or unimportant, just that Mr Deery talks A LOT. Like all day. I can't possibly remember all the good stuff he teaches us.

Mr Deery looks up at me from under his bushy eyebrows. 'So I think it's a great idea, Mac, and I think it's amazing that you want to help the teachers and the kids and the school, but I don't know if I can be in it. I'm sorry.'

'What?!' I yell. I didn't think for one second that Mr D would be the weak link. 'But . . . but you always tell us not to take stuff lying down – to fight for what we believe in. Was it all just talk?'

'No, not at all. It's just that I . . . I have a little . . . well, stage fright. Actually really bad stage fright. I just freeze up.'

'But you stand up in front of thirty kids every day.'

He shakes his head. 'It's not the same thing.'

I stare at Mr Deery, but he won't make eye contact. 'Is *that* why you made this a secret society?' I'd forgotten Mr Deery was the only one who never explained his reason for keeping this group on the down-low.

He just shrugs. 'I love musicals, so much. But the thought of being on stage makes me want to curl up in a ball and disappear.'

I can't imagine Mr Deery having stage fright. It's like hearing Ms Fox being called Mali. I never thought much about teachers as real people before. You know, with feelings and fears and stuff.

Flynn's hand goes up in the air. 'I know. Stop. Why don't you gherkin direct? I mean, we need a gherkin director, right? Whoop. And I can't think of anyone stop better.'

Mr Deery's head flicks up. 'Now, that I can do! Is that okay with you, Mac?'

'Of course,' I say.

Relief washes over Mr Deery's face. 'Perfect! Then I'm all in. So what's next?'

'Well,' I say, pulling a list out of my bag. Flynn and I wrote down all the things we could think of while we ate our burgers. 'Here's what we need to do to start . . .' I read out the list.

CHOOSE A MUSICAL

1) Ask ~~Mrs Heckleston~~ Jennifer if we can use Balthazar Theatre for rehearsals and the performance
2) Hold auditions (five people is probably not going to be enough to cast an entire musical)
3) Get a band together
4) Advertise the musical everywhere
5) Sell tickets
6) Perform to a sold-out crowd
7) Donate all the money made from the tickets to stop the Arts Fiasco at Watterson Primary

'Arts Fiasco?' says Mr Deery.

'It's what Mr Hubbard called it,' I explain.

'Ah yes, I should have guessed. Very theatrical!'

Binita snatches the list out of my hand. 'You call *that* a plan?' She scoffs at me and shoves our list into her briefcase. 'Leave it with me. I'll create an Excel spreadsheet, assign tasks and add it to a shared Google Drive folder that everyone can access.'

'A Google who?' asks Giuseppe.

Flynn pats him on the arm. 'Don't gherkin worry. I got you. Wheeee.'

Giuseppe shrugs and gives Flynn a thumbs-up.

'Well, I'm happy to talk to Jennifer about the theatre,' says Mr Deery. 'We might have to be a bit flexible in our schedule to work around whatever else she has going on, but I think she'll be fine with it.'

'Well then,' says Kathy. 'I guess we'd better get onto the most important item on that list. Which musical are we going to do?'

'Singin' in the Rain,' suggests Giuseppe without hesitation. 'I played Don Lockwood when I was a youngster. You shoulda seen me. Gene Kelly, eat your heart out.' He strikes a pose and flashes those

pearly whites. Seriously, it's like looking directly into car headlights.

Binita scoffs. 'All right, twinkle toes, let's see you dance up a lamp post in a walker.'

'Hey!' I say. 'You don't have to be rude, Binita. I bet Giuseppe could still dance circles around me. I dance like a confused jellyfish.'

'The jellyfish asks for directions to the hairdressers.' Everyone looks to Flynn, who shrugs. 'I don't know gherkin. Maybe he wanted his stop tentacles trimmed?'

We all burst out laughing. I make a mental note to write a song about that jellyfish for Stevie. He'd love it. Flynn's tics can be so unexpected and clever. The way he throws together words that might never see each other otherwise. It's pretty genius.

'Look,' says Mr Deery. 'How about we all come up with one suggestion for a musical and then we vote. But you can't vote for your own.'

Binita holds her phone in the air. '*Wicked* for me! I would be a brilliant Elphaba.'

Mr Deery jots it down. 'And Kathy?'

'Hmmmm, I'm gonna go old school and say *The Wizard of Oz*. That way Giuseppe can still dance up a storm as the Scarecrow and Binita can be the Wicked Witch of the West.'

Binita grins with pride but I'm not *entirely* sure Kathy meant it as a compliment.

'Flynn?'

'*Matilda* whoop! No gherkin question about it.'

'Surprise, surprise,' say Mr Deery with a grin. 'Okay, I'm going to go with *Annie*. And Mac?'

I think for a bit. I've never seen a real live musical before. This could be my first. Should I pick *Hairspray*? *Oliver!*? *Hello, Dolly!*? And then it hits me.

'*42nd Street*!'

Flynn grins at me. 'A show about gherkin putting on a show. Whoop! I love it.'

'Yes, very nice choice, Mac.' Mr Deery writes it down and then gives us all a piece of paper. 'Everyone write down your choice. Remember, you can't pick your own.'

We all hunch over our papers. I run the options through my head but it's not a hard choice. After listening to *Matilda* over and over again the other night, I love it just as much as Flynn does. I scribble *Matilda* down and hand my paper back to Mr D.

Once he has them all, he flicks through and then clears his throat before making the big announcement. 'The first production of the Secret Society of Broadway Musical Appreciation –'

'Ah, Mr D?' I interrupt. 'I think we might have to drop the "secret" part if we're going to put on a show.'

'Oh, yes, of course.' He clears his throat again. 'The first production of the Society of Broadway Musical Appreciation, aka SOBMA, will be . . . *MATILDA*!'

'Yes!' I jump to my feet, fists in the air. Flynn leaps up in excitement too.

'Matilda is my sister's foot doctor!' He shakes his head. 'She's not, but yay gherkin, whoop!'

Giuseppe and Binita give us a little clap, and Mr Deery and Kathy look on grinning.

Flynn grabs me by the shoulders. 'Not only are you whoop going to get to see your first gherkin musical, but you're stop going to be in it! Wheeee.'

Flynn's excitement is contagious, but a nervous energy bubbles up inside me. He gives my shoulders a shake. 'We're going to gherkin be in a musical, Mac! You are a gherkin genius stop. I can't wait to gherkin tell everybody. Wheeee.'

The bubbling stops and turns to a gurgle. Tell everybody? Uh oh. I know how much rehearsal this is going to take. I won't be able to keep up band practice AND do this. How am I going to break it to Mum that I'm dropping The Ants Pants to do a musical? This is *not* going to go down well.

I bolt home. Mum will go off at me for being late for sure. Saturday afternoon is dedicated family time. Non-negotiable. If we don't squeeze something in before she heads to The Garage for her shift, I'll never hear the end of it. On the upside, it's raining on me as I run down our street, so that means a family bike ride is out. Being late for indoor activities is not *as* bad.

I push through the front door, kick my boots off and shake myself dry onto the door mat.

Hearing the rock music blaring from the lounge room, I poke my head around the corner. Our dress-up box is open, clothes almost completely covering the lounge room floor. Stevie's hair has been gelled up into a mohawk and Mum has a well-worn blonde mullet wig on her head. Her phone is on its little bendy tripod legs and perched up on the mantlepiece.

Stevie screams the lyrics to 'School's Out' by Alice Cooper into a plastic microphone while sticking his face right up into the phone's camera. Mum rocks out proudly in the background on Stevie's rainbow keyboard. How a five-year-old who can barely remember to put undies on under his pants can remember all the lyrics to a song written like a century before he was born is totally beyond me, but Stevie's nailing it.

I just watch, smiling at my weird little family, until Mum calls, 'CUT!'

'Sorry I'm late,' I say, heading into the lounge room.

'Late, mate, shut the gate,' sings Stevie.

Mum picks up a flannel shirt and throws it at me. 'As punishment, you don't get to put anything in the song box, so expect a lot of indie pop.'

She rolls her eyes towards Stevie, who just chants softly, '"Dance Monkey", "Dance Monkey".'

Stevie grabs my hand and drags me over to the boxes on the table. 'You can choose next, Mac.'

We've been playing Family MTV since before Stevie was born, but he still thinks he runs the game.

I reach into the song box and swirl my hand around the folded-up bits of paper, grabbing one at random. Unfolding it, I read the song . . .

'"Gypsy" by Fleetwood Mac.' I glare at Mum. 'Gee, wonder who wrote this one? And you complain about Stevie's Tones and I overload.' I jab my thumb towards Stevie, who is already busy picking his next outfit.

Mum shrugs. 'I can't help that I know what perfect music is and stick to it.'

'Sure. But it wouldn't hurt to, you know, try some other stuff sometimes.'

'I do!' she says, looking at me like I've insulted her. 'I was just listening to The Cranberries this morning.'

'Mum! I mean OTHER kinds of music.'

'What, like . . . pop music?' she says, screwing her nose up.

'Or other stuff,' I say, dropping my head a little.

'Not classical?!' Mum looks horrified.

'Sure. Or something else, even. Like, I dunno, Broadway musicals?'

Mum stares at me for a second like she's not sure who I am and then bursts out laughing. *'Broadway musicals?'* she manages between laughs. 'I think I'd rather give my eyeballs paper cuts and squeeze lemon juice in them. Does that even count as music?' She wipes her eyes and tries to stop laughing. 'Nice one, Mac. Broadway musicals!'

I laugh along nervously. 'Yeah, funny, huh?'

'Hilarious!' She passes me the instrument box. 'Now, draw your instrument and grab a costume so we can get one more family music video in before I have to leave for work.'

I pull out a piece of paper and open it. 'Bass guitar.'

'Perfect!' says Mum, grabbing her own piece. 'Oh, look who's the lead singer.' She waves the paper at me, grinning.

Stevie draws keyboard and we set up. Mum selects 'Gypsy' on her phone and we play along as she sings. I usually love Family MTV, but today my heart's just not in it.

I can't stop thinking about SOBMA and our musical and about quitting the band as Mum perfectly imitates Stevie Nicks into the phone's camera. Soon, with the live music venue at work being turned into a pokies room, she's not going to have anywhere to sing except our lounge room. Mum doesn't need any more bad news right now. I think I'll keep that extra 'S' in front of SOBMA for the time being and let it stay a secret. From Mum at least. For her own sake.

ACT TWO

Scene Three

Balthazar Theatre

Mac wanders through the foyer of the theatre, looking at all the posters of previous productions. He runs his hand along the creators' names at the bottom, dreaming that one day he too will see his name on a poster.

'I Just Can't Wait to Be a Star'

(to the tune of 'I Just Can't Wait to Be King' from *The Lion King*)

I'm gonna be a mighty star
So Broadway get prepared.
Well, I've never been on stage before
But I'm not all that scared.
I'm gonna be a superstar
Like no kid was before.

I'll make a mint, I'll sign my name
The crowd will yell for more!
Some might think I'm taking it too far
But I just can't wait to be a star.

No one saying 'play rock'
No one saying 'sing that'
No one saying 'be cool'
No one saying 'what's that?'.
Free to play my songs all day.
Free to sing things all my way!

'Hi, Mac.'

I spin around at the sound of a voice I barely recognise. Flynn gives me a small wave.

'Hey, Flynn. Are you okay?' He doesn't look like himself at all. He reminds me of Stevie's robot toy when the batteries are running low.

'Yeah,' he says. 'Just whoop a bit of a gherkin . . . morning.' I follow him through the theatre. He takes a seat at the piano but doesn't even open the lid.

Usually, Flynn can't be near the piano for more than two seconds without tapping on the keys. Something is definitely wrong. It's like someone stole the . . . Flynn out of him.

He raises his head. 'Do you gherkin know why Mr Deery wanted to whoop meet us?' he asks.

'Nope. He should be here soon.'

We sit for a bit, saying nothing. Just the sound of Flynn's tics filling the silence every now and then. I know something's not right, but maybe it's Flynn's business. Maybe he doesn't want to talk about it. Then again, Flynn said he'd rather I ask questions. I don't know a lot about being a good friend but if he doesn't want to talk about it, I think he'll tell me. So . . .

'Do you wanna tell me what's wrong, Flynn?'

He gives me the rude finger and then covers it with his other hand. 'That's what's gherkin wrong!' he says. 'My stupid whoop tics.'

I'm a bit shocked. I've never heard Flynn hate on his tics before. 'I don't care,' I say. 'You can give me a million rude fingers. I know it's a tic.'

Flynn sighs. 'You do. Stop. Not everybody gherkin does.'

I slide next to Flynn on the piano seat. 'What happened?'

'This gherkin morning, I was just walking down the whoop street, thinking about the gherkin musical and I passed some stop guy. I gherkin yelled out "stick the breadstick up your whoop nose" and did my stop rude finger tic. Give the bin the bird!

'Of course it wasn't gherkin at him, but next thing I know wheeee he's yelling at me for gherkin picking a fight. Whoop.' Flynn rubs his eyes. He looks really shook up. 'He was all up in my wheeee face, screaming, but I barely even gherkin realised what I'd said.'

'You're kidding!' I say. 'Did you explain your Tourette's?'

Flynn rolls his eyes at me. 'This wasn't the whoop kind of guy who gherkin waits around for an explanation. Wheeee. Plus, I was so stop scared that my tics kicked into gherkin overdrive. Bucket on your head. Eventually I gherkin freaked him out enough that he just whoop left.'

I feel terrible and don't know what to say. I don't know if there *is* anything to say. I wish Mr Piddles was here, he always makes Flynn happy. But I'm ferret-less . . . and solution-less.

I do the only thing I can. I sit with my friend. 'What's wrong with people?'

Flynn shrugs. 'Most of the gherkin time I'm okay with my stop Tourette's. Then some days whoop it just really sucks, you know? Gherkin.'

I don't know. I guess nobody really knows what it's like to be Flynn except Flynn. But I'm trying my best to understand. 'I'm so sorry, Flynn. Are you okay?'

He gives me a small smile. 'I will be. Whoop.'

'Hey guys.' Mr Deery bursts through the theatre doors and jogs down the aisle to the stage. 'The others can't make it, but I wanted to give you the news face to face.' Mr Deery stops in his tracks and stares at Flynn. 'You okay, Flynn?'

Flynn waves it off. 'What's the whoop news?'

Mr Deery hands us a piece of paper. 'I researched the cost of the rights to perform a musical. *Matilda* can't be licensed to community theatre at all and the others are all so expensive. There's just no way we can afford it. I'm sorry. It's a really great idea, Mac, it is. We can't do it without licensing the rights first, though, and I can't see how that's possible.'

I look down at the paper in my hands. It's a printout with money amounts on it that have more zeroes than I've ever seen before.

'*That* much?' I say.

Mr Deery nods.

'Wow!' I stare at all those zeroes. 'There's gotta be something we can do. Flynn?'

I look to him for help but he just shrugs defeatedly.

'Mr Deery?' He's focused on Flynn. I try again. 'Maybe we could tweet Tim Minchin? I mean he seems like a pretty cool guy. Maybe he'd let us perform *Matilda* for free.'

Mr Deery puts his hand on my shoulder. 'It doesn't quite work like that, Mac. I'm sure Mr Minchin would love to help us out, but he doesn't exactly own the musical and he might be a bit busy to see our tweet.'

I turn back to Flynn. He doesn't look like he has any fight in him.

'I'm really sorry, kids,' says Mr Deery. 'Maybe we can come up with a different idea. A garage sale or something?'

I know Mr D is trying to help, but a garage sale is a sucky idea.

'Look, I have to go. We'll put our heads together and come up with something.' He hands a USB to Flynn. 'I loved the song, Flynn, so much. Maybe you could play it for Mac?'

Flynn passes the USB to me. 'Here. You can gherkin listen, if you want. Wheeee.'

Mr Deery gives Flynn one more concerned look. 'Are you sure you're okay?'

I watch Flynn as he taps his fingers softly on the piano lid. I really want him to talk to Mr Deery, but it's his call.

Flynn lifts his head. 'I had another gherkin . . . run-in.'

Mr Deery's face changes immediately. 'What happened?'

Flynn tells his story again and I can see Mr D's doing his best to stay calm, but the way his lower jaw is clenching tells me he's failing epically.

'Was it the same guy?' Mr Deery asks. Flynn shakes his head. 'Have you told your parents?'

'Not gherkin yet.'

'But you will?'

'Yeah. When I get whoop home. Just want to gherkin hang out with stop Mac a bit first.'

Mr Deery nods. 'I understand. Can I call your dad? Maybe we can all chat tonight?'

'Sure. Whoop!' Flynn gives him a small smile. 'Can you bring gherkin pizza? Minus the stop gherkin, of course.'

Mr Deery smiles. 'Always! You sure you'll be okay, Flynn?'

'Don't worry, Mr D, I got him,' I say.

He nods. 'Okay. Call me if you need anything, all right? I'll see you tonight.'

Flynn waves goodbye and Mr Deery leaves.

'No gherkin musical. Well, that wheeee news just topped off an awesome whoop day, didn't it? Life sucks on a dirty sock,' says Flynn.

'Hey!' I say, jumping up and grabbing Flynn's arm. 'I've got an idea! Something that might take your mind off things.'

'I dunno, Mac. I'm stop not really in the gherkin mood.'

'We're friends, right?'

'Of course. Wheeee.'

'Do you trust me?'

Flynn nods and gives me the rude finger. 'Sorry.'

'No apologising. If you trust me, then come.'

Flynn pulls himself up off the piano stool and lets me drag him out of the theatre.

'Where are you gherkin taking me, Mac?' Flynn asks as we pass the edge of town.

'Almost there. It'll be worth it, I promise.'

Flynn stands on the back pegs of my bike as we round the street corner to see a big property set back a bit off the road. I pull up out in front. Flynn jumps off and I dump the bike. A small house sits at the front of the block. Though house is probably a bit generous – it's more like a shack.

'Ah, are you trying to gherkin kidnap me, Mac? Whoop. Are we stop going to save Ms gherkin Fox's job with ransom money?'

'I'm thinking about it,' I say, dragging Flynn towards the house. I knock on the door and we wait. Finally, Slater opens the door.

'Mac, little dude. What's up?' He gives me a fist bump and turns to Flynn. 'Who's this?'

'Slater, this is my friend Flynn. Flynn, Slater. He plays drums in one of the bands at Mum's work.'

'Used to,' says Slater, running his hand through some pretty out-of-control hair. Slater has mastered the art of permanently looking like he's just woken up. 'You heard about the pokies thing, right?'

'Yeah,' I say. 'Total bummer.'

Flynn tics a few times next to me and Slater throws him a look. I can see Flynn doesn't have an explanation in him today.

'Hey, Slater, can we have a look around?'

Slater throws open the door. 'Course, little man, any time. You know the rules.'

'Thanks.' I walk on through the shack, Flynn close behind. As we step out the back door and into the giant yard, Slater yells at us.

'I haven't done the feeds yet, so feel free. Just let me know who you do.'

'Okay!' I yell back, letting the door close behind us.

'Wow,' says Flynn, looking around. 'What is this gherkin place?'

Standing at the back door, there are aviaries to our left and some huts and pens on the right. The backyard spreads out before us, divided into different coops, tanks and fenced-off areas. Then behind that, stretching into the distance, is a long paddock.

'It's an animal rescue/sanctuary/boarding house sort of thing. Slater is a *big* fan of animals. He's a good friend of Mum's and lets me come and hang out here when I want. I've seen how Mr Piddles sort of Zens you out, so I thought maybe a bit of an animal-hangout session might improve a crappy day?'

A huge smile spreads across Flynn's face. 'You mean we can gherkin play with them? Whoop. Like stop, any of them?'

'Yup.'

He looks at me with excitement and I can see the old Flynn creeping back. 'Does he have any gherkin ferrets?'

'Sure does. This is actually where Mr Piddles came from.'

We walk through the yard, stopping to visit with different animals along the way. We give the turtles some mushrooms and a few leaves of spinach and I mark the feed off on the chart hanging in front of their tank. Flynn takes some lettuce out of the bucket and holds it for the rabbits to nibble on. I can see him starting to relax, the stress of the morning lifting from him like steam off a cooling lasagne.

'Better?' I ask.

He grins. 'So much gherkin better. Thanks, Mac.'

There are some blue heeler puppies in one of the pens, so I change out their water and clean up a bit while Flynn lies on the ground and lets them roll all over him, nibbling on his ears and treading on his face. There's nothing like a puppy attack for anyone who needs cheering up. Within fifteen minutes of being at Slater's, Flynn is back to his old self. I always thought Flynn's Tourette's didn't bother him, but I guess we all have good and bad days.

'Flynn! Over here.'

He reluctantly crawls out from under the pile of blue heelers and squeezes out of the pen, shutting the gate quickly behind him before the flood of puppies can escape.

We make our way into the ferret hutch and I pass a little white one to Flynn.

'Stop it!' he squeals as he holds her up to his nose and she nibbles on it. 'So cute!'

'That's Lulu,' I explain. 'I thought you might like her.'

Flynn sits down cross-legged on the ground as Lulu sniffs her way up his arm and behind his neck, inspecting him carefully.

'Looks like Lulu likes you,' I say, playing with a larger ferret. 'And maybe the feeling is mutual?'

'Yeah,' agrees Flynn as Lulu makes her way down into his lap. He crosses his legs tighter, creating a space for her to curl up. 'I've always wanted a gherkin pet, but with us always moving it just wasn't whoop possible. Since we moved here, I've been bugging Mum and Dad. Wheeee. No luck yet though. They wanted to see whether I gherkin settled into school and stuff first.'

'Is it hard?' I ask. 'High school? 'Cos I'm pretty nervous about it.'

Flynn shrugs. 'It has its moments. Probably a bit gherkin easier without the Tourette's, I imagine.' He smiles at me, patting an almost asleep Lulu. 'You'll be fine. Plus you'll have gherkin me.'

'Are you sure you'll hang out with me at high school?' I ask softly. 'You know, with me being the year below and everything.'

Flynn laughs. 'Are you sure you'll hang out with gherkin ME? The kid with whoop Tourette's?'

I so don't think of Flynn that way. There's nothing I want more than for him to be my friend in high school. 'Let's make a deal. Friends forever, no matter what high school brings.'

'You've got a gherkin deal!' he says and we shake on it.

That night, I lie in bed staring at my glow-in-the-dark stars. I copied Flynn's song off the USB he gave me onto my iPhone and it now streams through my earphones into my brain. It's the seventh time I've listened to it. I can't believe a twelve-year-old wrote it. He must be some kind of musical prodigy. I'm not just saying that 'cos he's my friend either, I swear. This song is the kind of music that goes straight through your ears and into your heart. It warms you up, kinda like when you drink the leftover liquid from two-minute noodles.

I imagine Flynn's fingers bouncing across the piano keys. His face with that small sideways smile he gets when he plays, like he knows a secret that you don't. His head slightly tilted to the right in concentration.

'MAC!'

I sit up, pulling out my earphones to see Stevie standing in my bedroom doorway.

'I called your name a hundred times,' he says, sulking a little.

'Sorry, Stevie, I was listening to some music. What's up?'

He scurries over to my bed and climbs up next to me. 'Moshie's dreams are getting louder than *Bluey*.'

After dinner and dishes, I'd left Stevie in front of *Bluey* and Mrs Moshie sleeping in the armchair as usual. But if Stevie has stopped watching *Bluey* without being dragged kicking and screaming away from the TV, then Mrs Moshie must be making some serious noise.

'What you listening to?' asks Stevie.

'My friend wrote a song on the piano.'

'What friend?' Stevie grabs at my earphones.

'His name's Flynn. You haven't met him.' I put one earphone in Stevie's ear and one in mine. 'Here, you wanna listen?'

He nods and crosses his legs.

I press play. Stevie listens intensely for a while, then looks up at me. 'It's got no words.'

I nod. 'Yeah, Flynn just plays the piano and writes music.'

'But I like music with words.'

'I know, Stevie, but a song has to start somewhere. This one starts with the music.'

Stevie pulls the earphone out and tosses it at me, unimpressed. 'You should give him some words.' He jumps up and heads for the door, pulling it shut behind him.

I lean back against my bedhead and stare at the earphone in my lap. I know Stevie's only five, but that's actually a brilliant idea – I reckon Flynn would love that. When I'm feeling down, listening to songs that mean something to me really helps. Maybe if Flynn has his very own song, it'll help him through the crappy times too.

I grab a notebook and a pen. I'm gonna write Flynn a song. Just for him. I press play. The music dances through my head again, but this time words attach themselves to the notes and my hand scribbles them down.

Monday drags by sooooooooo slowly. I just want to go meet Flynn and show him his song. At least the last class today is extension music.

Extension music is something Ms Fox created all on her own. It's part of a Year Five and Six elective program, so kids who have an extra special interest in art or music or whatever can spend a bit more time on stuff we might not cover in normal music class.

Extension music is kind of how The Ants Pants started. Toby Baker from Year Five joined the class, Ms Fox teamed us up with the Ledden twins and before we knew it, we had a band! We got put together 'cos we all liked rock music. There's also a string quartet with the violin and cello kids, and a composers' group who spend most of the class glued to Garage Band.

If Ms Fox goes, extension music goes too.

I haven't come up with a new idea to save Ms Fox yet. I really thought the musical was the perfect solution – save the arts with the arts! But Mr D says he just can't see a way around the licensing issue. I get it, I do. Paying rights for stuff is super important – that's how artists get paid. But it also sucks, you know, when you're an eleven-year-old kid who just wants to help his favourite teacher.

I run through the front doors of Balthazar Theatre and straight into Kathy. 'Whoa there, Flash Gordon!' says Kathy, catching Mr Piddles as he almost tumbles off her shoulder. 'Where's the fire?'

'Huh? Who's Gordon?'

Kathy rolls her eyes at me. 'Never mind, just slow down. You almost scared the whiskers off Mr Piddles.'

'Sorry, Mr Piddles.' I give the ferret a rub under the chin while he eyes me suspiciously. 'What are you doing here, Kathy? Do we have a meeting?'

'No. Jennifer's assistant is on holidays so I'm helping her out with some of the books and things.'

'Really?' I'm trying not to sound too unconvinced, but Kathy doesn't really strike me as the accountant-y type.

She screws up her nose at me. 'I'll have you know I was top of my class at Watterson Primary.'

'Sure thing.' I look around. 'Is Jennifer here? Flynn's coming and we wanted to use the theatre for a little bit, if that's okay?'

Kathy heads over to the snack counter and pulls out a big blue diary. 'She's dealing with some issue in the bathrooms.' Grabbing a red ribbon that hangs out the bottom of the diary, Kathy flips it open. 'There's a bump-in at seven, but I'm sure she won't mind if you use it until then.'

'What's a bump-in?' I ask.

'Oh, just a bit of theatre lingo,' Kathy explains. 'It's when you move all the set and everything in for a show. Don't worry, we'll have you talking like a thespian in no time.'

'Like a what?'

Kathy laughs. 'Never mind. Point is, you can use it!'

I peer at the scribble on the pages. Things crossed out and re-written and re-written again. It looks like a disorganised mess to me. Haven't they heard of Google Calendar?

A bang comes from the bathroom as Jennifer, wearing wet overalls, comes striding out. 'I've fixed it for now, but we should probably get Maya out here to take a look soon.' She wipes her hands on a towel. 'Hey, Mac, what are you doing here?'

'Flynn and I were hoping to squeeze in for an hour if that's okay?'

Jennifer looks to Kathy, who gives her a thumbs-up. 'All clear until seven.'

'That's when the bump-in starts,' I say, winking at Kathy.

She nods back. 'Fast learner!'

'Off you go then.' Jennifer waves me in. 'Tell Flynn to take it easy on those keys.'

'Thanks!' I wave to them both and head into the theatre.

I've barely settled in when the doors fly open again. 'Hey, hey there whoop, Mr Mac gherkin!'

Flynn skips in looking pumped.

'Hey,' I say, giving him a fist bump. 'You look good.'

He runs his hand through his hair doing his best Danny-from-*Grease* impression. 'It's a gherkin curse being this good-looking whoop!'

Flynn takes a seat at the piano and flicks it open. Locking his fingers together, he stretches his arms out in front of him. 'Whoop!' His fingers dance across the keys as he taps out a quick rendition of 'The Nicest Kids in Town' from *Hairspray*. He stops and turns to me. 'That one was for gherkin you, Mac. Wheeee!'

'Why thank you. And now, I have a little, I dunno, surprise for you?'

'Surprises make the lizard poop! Ha! I love gherkin surprises. What is it stop?'

I pull out my notebook. 'So you know that song you wrote? Well, I loved it. Like, *really* loved it. And I kinda wrote some words to it. I hope you don't mind?'

'Mind? Whoop! That's the coolest gherkin present ever.' Flynn swings himself back around to face the piano. 'Let's gherkin hear it!'

Suddenly, I'm super nervous. You know that feeling where you're really excited and sure about something until the moment comes that you have to share it outside of your own head – share it out loud – to another person? And then all that certainty you felt just falls away, leaving you feeling kind of bare? Yup, that's the feeling I have right now.

And Flynn sees it.

'It's cool, dude. Stop. Safe space here whoop! I'm gonna gherkin love it.' He gives me that reassuring Flynn-grin and starts to play the intro.

His fingers bounce along the piano exactly like I imagined and the melody sounds even better live than it did on the recording. I look at Flynn and he's lost in the piano. I brush aside all the doubt and focus on the page in front of me. The one titled 'Flynn's Song'.

```
A clock without its tick means it
isn't workin'
```

A rollercoaster's no fun without a bit
of jerkin'
You wouldn't be the same Flynn
if you lost your gherkin
It's part of you
And we love it all

A milkshake's just boring milk if you
lose the shakin'
We love the awesome puns that you're
always makin'
Like 'fried eggs with a side of
Kevin Bacon'
It's part of you
And we love it all

So when the jerks have got you down
Don't you forget that
The ones who count have got your back
'Cos I'm dead set that
I wouldn't change a single thing
And don't regret that
You are you
And we love it all.

When I finish, I look up from my page. Flynn's hands rest lightly on the piano. He slowly looks up at me and I can see his eyes are sort of wet. Oh crap, I made him cry! Did he take it the wrong way? Did I upset him? That's not what I meant at all.

'Are you okay, Flynn?'

He shakes his head.

'Why?'

He rubs his eyes. 'Because I just heard the best gherkin song ever written in the history of stop songs. And it was for gherkin me.'

'Well, I just wrote the words. You wrote the music. So I think we can officially say it was a team effort.'

Flynn looks at me for a bit without saying anything, then smiles. 'Thanks, Mac.'

'For the song? No worries.'

'Nah, just for gherkin getting it.'

I'm not entirely sure what it is I 'get' but he looks happy. So I'm happy.

'And you're right stop,' says Flynn. 'We make a great gherkin team. Like Batman and Robin. Wheeee!'

'Or Rodgers and Hammerstein.'

'Who?'

I throw my hands in the air. 'C'mon. Richard Rodgers and Oscar Hammerstein? The most famous musical duo ever. They wrote *Oklahoma!*, *The King and I* and *The Sound of Music*. You MUST have heard of them. Rodgers wrote the music and Hammerstein wrote the lyrics. How can you be in a broadway musical appreciation society and NOT know Rodgers and Hammerstein?'

'Mac! You're a gherkin genius!'

'Not really,' I say. 'They're pretty well known.'

Flynn grabs me by the shoulders. 'No, I mean you've gherkin solved our stop problem. We don't need to license the rights to a whoop musical.'

'We don't?'

'No!' A huge smile spreads across his face. 'We're going to gherkin write our own. Whoop!'

'We are?'

Flynn shakes me. 'Mac! Watterson has its very own gherkin Rodgers and stop Hammerstein. You and gherkin me. We're going to whoop write a musical, stop the Arts gherkin Fiasco and save the entire wheeee arts program of Watterson Primary.'

I stare at him. How are two kids going to write an entire musical? He's got to be kidding, right? I mean it's totally impossible!

'Are you gherkin in or are you whoop in?'

He looks so excited. How can I possibly say no to that face?

'I'm in.'

'WOOHOO!' yells Flynn, jumping onto the piano stool. 'Flynn has saved the gherkin day. Pay for the show in peanuts!'

I laugh as I watch him bow to an imaginary audience. He looks seriously happy with himself. I decide to wait until later to break it to him that there's no way I can write an entire musical.

Absolutely no way.

Apparently Mr Deery disagrees, because he thinks it's a brilliant idea.

And he can't wait to tell the rest of SOBMA.

Back at Balthazar, he introduces us as 'Flynn Rodgers and Mac Hammerstein'. All of SOBMA – plus Jennifer, who's been dragged into the meeting – listen as I outline the very brief plan.

'So Flynn thought we could write our own musical, and that way the rights won't be a problem,' I explain nervously.

They all love it –

'Brilliant!'

'Perfect!'

'Squeak!'

– Giuseppe and Kathy and even Mr Piddles. Binita doesn't really think any ideas other than her own are brilliant, but she does look up from her phone for at least 3.5 seconds and gives an agreeing shrug. That's about as close to a compliment as you're gonna get from Binita.

I keep waiting for someone to point out that we're just a couple of kids and there's no way we can write a whole musical, but apparently there isn't a single voice of reason in the whole group. Where's a cynical adult when you need one? Nope, our overly ambitious plan is put into immediate action. And by our next meeting everyone is all over it.

'I've scheduled an audition day,' says Mr Deery. 'I'm guessing we'll need some more people for the cast, and a chorus at the very least, right?'

'I've highlighted all the times the theatre will be unused in the diary and sent them to Binita,' Jennifer explains. 'You lot are welcome to use any unbooked times for rehearsals, and I've blocked out a week between two of our other shows for your performances.'

'I'm emailing you all a schedule,' Binita says to her phone, but I guess it's really directed at us. 'It covers rehearsals, bump-in, dress rehearsal and the performance run. It's all in the Google Calendar I've shared with everyone.' She rolls her eyes. 'And I'll print one for you, Giuseppe.'

'Don't you worry about that. Henry Wu's daughter showed me about the Goggle thing. I'm all over it.' Giuseppe looks pretty chuffed with himself, so I don't point out that it's Google not Goggle. 'I also spoke to my Scrabble group and got everyone on board to help. I've got builders and painters for the set, sewers for costumes and some excellent cooks for rehearsal snacks.'

'Great!' says Mr Deery. 'So that just leaves us with the actual musical.'

Everyone turns and stares expectantly at Flynn and me. I swallow loudly. You know it's not good when you can hear yourself swallow. I look at Flynn, but he doesn't seem to be experiencing the same feeling of fear and pressure that I am. Actually, he looks kinda stoked. Like he's ready to take on the world.

'No gherkin worries,' says Flynn confidently. 'Mac and I are locking ourselves in a gherkin metaphorical creative vault stop and you'll have a gherkin musical in no time whoop. Tap dancing chipmunks are loud!'

I don't know if that's entirely true. Not the 'tap dancing chipmunks' part – that could totally be true. The 'musical in no time' part. I mean, I'm going over to Flynn's house for a brainstorm and a writing session tomorrow but this all seems pretty unrealistic to me. According to the schedule, rehearsals start at the end of term – which is in four weeks. FOUR WEEKS! Even Lin-Manuel Miranda couldn't write a musical in four weeks!

Flynn clearly sees the fear in my eyes and pats my shoulder. 'Don't gherkin worry,' he says. 'We got this. Whoop!'

I dig Flynn's confidence, I really do, but we're just kids. We SO don't got this!

Flynn leans in and whispers. 'When you stop go to bed tonight, listen to gherkin "A Million Dreams" from whoop *The Greatest Showman*. I promise, we gherkin got this!'

He winks at me and leaves it there. Flynn has a song for everything.

ACT TWO

Scene Four

Flynn Vanderberg's House

Mac leans his bike against the fence and takes the house in. It's much bigger than his own. Much newer. He hovers in front, nervous to step into someone else's world and unsure that he really has what it takes to write a musical. FLYNN VANDERBERG's head pops through the top window as he sings down to Mac.

'Come Inside'

(to the tune of 'Come Alive' from *The Greatest Showman*)

You waste away your days
Playing what you're told
But there's a song in you.
Like a sun that hides its rays
You fit the mould
But you can break away.

'Cos you think that there's no straying
From the stuff you're always playing
But we can write a show and save the
town, just you and me.
Come on up, the world is waiting
You be you and no one's hating
What you find will blow your mind
You'll have to knock and see.

Come inside, come inside
Got a show to write, gotta join the fight.
Come on up, to the top
We can do it now, I will show you how.

When your dreams become reality
You know Broadway's where you wanna be
'Cos a musical, it lives inside you.
And you know that you are much more than
Just a player in a school rock band
'Cos a musical, it lives inside you.
So, come inside!

'Are you gonna gherkin come in?' yells Flynn from the top window. 'Or just stop hang around outside like a creep whoop? Wherefore art thou creepy waffle!'

I rub my hands together as I walk towards the door. I suddenly realise: I'm really nervous. I have no idea why. I guess I don't go round to other kids' houses that often. I hope I act the right way; remember my manners and everything. I take a deep breath and press the doorbell.

Before I even have time to remove my finger, the door swings open, revealing a tall guy with kind of longish hair, a moustache-beard thing that goes all the way round his mouth but nowhere near his ears and a giant cheesy grin.

'Mac!' he booms. 'Guitar playing, lyric-writing extraordinaire! Nice to finally meet you.'

Before I can respond, the man is gently pushed aside by a much shorter woman. Her haircut is almost the same as the man's but she has no mouth-circling moustache-beard. I wonder if they go to the same hairdresser.

'Sorry about him,' she says, shaking her head. 'He can be a little OTT sometimes.'

I pretend I know what OTT means and return her kind smile. 'Nice to meet you,' I say. 'I'm Mac.'

'I'm Remy and this joker is Levi.'

Flynn pushes between them. 'And I'm the long-suffering gherkin child of these wheeee two. Stop.'

Levi gives Flynn a squeeze. 'You poor thing, life is soooooooo tough with us.'

'Introductions whoop done. We're going to the gherkin music room wheeee.' Flynn grabs my arm and drags me off.

'But we've barely even spoken two words to Mac,' Remy calls after us.

'You can grill him at gherkin lunch. Put the lamp post on the barbeque.'

I wave over my shoulder at them as Flynn drags me through a door and downstairs.

'We probably should have at least stayed and –'

Whhhhooooooaaaa! I stop at the bottom of the stairs and take it all in.

The room looks like a real-life recording studio. Not that I've ever actually seen a real-life recording studio, but Mum has shown me photos of the one her band used when she was younger. We've also watched that Fleetwood Mac documentary Mum loves (like a thousand times) and this room pretty much looks like a modern-day version of that.

There are instruments everywhere and computers with lots of big screens. On either side of a huge desk are sound decks covered in knobs and dials and slide-y things – I have no idea what any of them do. An electric keyboard is plugged into one of the computers and cables run back and forth connecting it all together. On one side of the room is a box that look like a shopping centre change room but with walls made of mattresses. Okay, maybe they're not literally mattress-walls but they sure look like it. Inside the box stands a microphone behind a large circle that looks like thick flyscreen. It's just like those places megastars go to record their chart-topping hits.

'This is awesome!' I say, slowly spinning around one more time to take it all in.

'Yeah, it's pretty gherkin cool,' agrees Flynn. 'It's the upside to stop having parents who whoop work in the gherkin music industry.'

‘What do they *actually* do?’ I ask, wondering if Flynn’s family could possibly get ANY more awesome.

‘Dad was a gherkin performer and Mum was a stop stage manager. They met on a wheeee performance of gherkin *My Fair Lady*. So cheesy.’

Yep, they just got awesome-er.

‘So they *both* worked on actual, real-life musicals?’

Flynn nods. ‘Until we moved to gherkin Watterson so I could get a stop proper education. In Watterson gherkin of all places! Whoop.’

‘Where did you go to school before?’

‘Gherkin home school. Well, technically gherkin theatre school wheeee. We were stop always on the gherkin road with shows. Now Mum and Dad stop work from home. Music gherkin production stuff. Whoop.’

I shake my head in disbelief. I am standing in the house of real, legit musical theatre people. I spot a wall covered in programs and head over to take a look. *Chicago*, *The Lion King*, *Cats*, *Les Mis*,

Rent, *Fiddler on the Roof*, *Grease*, *In the Heights*, *Hair*, *The Sound of Music*, *Avenue Q*, *The Wizard of Oz*, *School of Rock*. You name a musical, it's on the wall.

'Have your parents seen ALL of these?' I ask.

Flynn laughs. 'They've gherkin DONE all of these. Stop. These are the programs of every gherkin show they've worked on. Whoop. And I've gherkin been to them all. Stop.'

My head swims. I imagine little baby Flynn crawling down the yellow brick road or getting a piggy-back ride from Pumbaa.

'You must be the luckiest kid on the planet,' I say, thinking about what an awesome playground musical theatre must be.

Flynn bursts out laughing.

'What?' I turn to him. 'Seriously! You've had the best life. I'd switch with you in a second.'

He laughs again. 'Well, that's a gherkin first. Not sure anyone stop has ever wanted to whoop switch lives with me before. Wheeee.'

'Really?' I say. 'I can't imagine anyone NOT wanting to.'

'I think you gherkin might be looking at things stop through Broadway-tinted glasses, Mac! Whoop.'

I turn back to the programs. 'Hey, maybe your parents could help us with our musical? I know Mr D has a whole bunch of faith in us, but I just don't see the two of us writing a *whole* musical, especially in only four weeks.'

Flynn jumps up and heads over to one of the giant computer screens. 'Well, actually stop, that's what I wanted to gherkin show you.'

Flynn clicks through a couple of folders and finally gets to one that says 'Flynn's Masters' and opens it up. There's a whole heap of WAV files in there. They aren't named, just numbered. It looks like there's about forty of them.

'What are they?' I ask.

'Just some stuff I've gherkin put together over the stop years.' Flynn double clicks on one of the files and a song plays through the four speakers circling our heads. I recognise it straight away. Not like, I can name the song, but I know the feel. It's got to be one of Flynn's.

'Did you write this?'

He nods.

I look at the folder again. 'Did you write ALL of these?'

He nods again.

'Flynn, are you some kind of child prodigy Mozart type?

Flynn laughs. 'Nah. Just a gherkin kid who likes writing stop music and has way too much gherkin time on his hands. Whoop! I thought maybe we could gherkin go through these and pick out some for the wheeee musical. Then we come up with a stop storyline and you write the gherkin lyrics. Abracadabra instant musical noodles!'

I take over the mouse and click on another song. It's as good as the first – maybe better.

'Flynn, with all this, we're pretty much halfway there.'

'Yup. Whoop. And I have gherkin sheet music for all of these stop too.'

'You're amazing!'

'Hardly gherkin.'

I shake my head at him. 'No, seriously! There's so much here to work with. Now we just have to decide what the musical is about.'

'Where do we gherkin even start? Whoop!'

'Well, there's a few options, I guess. We could base it on a book, like *Oliver!* or *Les Mis*.'

'Wouldn't we have more gherkin rights issues with that? Wheeee.'

'Yeah, good point. Okay, so there's a lot of love stories out there, you know, *West Side Story*, *Hello, Dolly!*, *Funny Girl*.'

'Love story? Gherkin. Meh, so overdone. I love toast!'

'Totally overdone. What about the old rags to riches thing? We could have a character who starts out unsuccessful and becomes a big success?'

Flynn screws up his nose. 'I dunno. Whoop. Success is gherkin so subjective.'

'So what?'

'Like it means different gherkin things to different people stop.'

I drum my fingers on the mouse pad. 'How about we hit up the internet for some inspiration.' I type 'what should I write about' into Google and scan through the results. 'The most popular suggestion seems to be "write about something you know".'

Flynn scoffs. 'Oh great, a gherkin musical about stop homework and chores. Whoop. Sounds super gherkin exciting.'

'Ha! Well, what about some of the cool stuff that's happened around here? We could write about those kids at my school who found a million bucks and caught that criminal. Or how about that big take-down of the old mayor a few months ago? That was pretty cool. And not every town has someone living in a Lego house in the middle of their park. I mean, for such a boring town, some pretty cool stuff happens in Watterson. Maybe we could write a musical about one of those?'

Flynn stops, almost still. He gives me some rock hands and his eyes widen. 'Or we could whoop write about gherkin all of them.'

'Huh?'

'You're gherkin brilliant, Mac. Nothing could be easier to wheeee write, easier to cast stop or easier to sell gherkin tickets to. It's perfect!'

'What's perfect?'

Flynn flashes a huge grin.

'Watterson: The gherkin *Musical!'*

'Watterson: The Musical,' I repeat slowly. A musical about our town, the people in it and the bizarre things that always seem to happen here.

Maybe Flynn is right. Maybe I AM a genius.

Within a couple of hours we have a list of possible characters and events that might make it into our musical.

POSSIBLE CHARACTERS/STORYLINES:

1) Tess Heckleston and Toby Baker – two kids find a million dollars in their backyard and go on a big spending spree.
2) Scotty the Criminal – Watterson's resident bad guy who gets busted by local kids.
3) 'Kooky' Kathy – town mascot who lives in Brennan Park in her Lego house.
4) Mr Piddles – Kathy's ferret sidekick.
5) The Green Peas (original members Casey, Cookie and Zeke) – a group of kids who expose and take down the dodgy town mayor.

6) Ex-mayor Lupphol – the dodgy ex town mayor.
7) Mayor Wu – new (and totally un-dodgy) town mayor.
8) Mrs Keiren – permanently grumpy school principal.
9) Senior Detective McKenzie – the one who's always around to slap the handcuffs on the baddies . . . after the kids of the town seem to do most of the hard work.
10) Mr D – school teacher, loved by all.

'Wow!' I say, looking over the list. 'We really do have quite the cast here at Watterson. With everything this lot has been up to, a storyline shouldn't be too difficult to pull together.'

'Yeah, this gherkin place is whacky whoop.' Flynn points to the next page. 'Go through the settings.'

POSSIBLE SETTINGS:

1) Watterson Primary School – easy to create on stage, just need some desks from school – ask Mr D to ~~steal~~ borrow them.

2) Brennan Park – get some trees, maybe a park bench. Could we temporarily move Kathy's Lego house into the theatre for the show?
3) Town Hall/Mayor's Office – if what Zeke says about sneaking into the mayor's office is true, this would make an awesome scene for the musical.
4) Patty's Burger Barn or The Funky Anchovy – the only two ~~decent~~ restaurants in Watterson.
5) Balthazar Theatre – a theatre set in a theatre that is that theatre.
6) Watto Mall – just 'cos everyone goes there. It's pretty much the only place to go. For anything.

'Okay,' says Flynn, looking over our list, 'this all looks gherkin great but how are we going to stop tie it all together?'

'Maybe we could have a narrator or something?' I suggest. 'Like in *Joseph and the Amazing Technicolor Dreamcoat*? Someone who kinda tells us the story of Watterson and leads us through its history?'

'How far back are we gherkin going to go? Whoop.'

'Way back,' I say. 'Like the whole of this year, I reckon. That way we can cover all the really cool stuff.'

'Gherkin awesome.' Flynn runs his pen down our character list. 'Question is, who should our gherkin narrator be whoop?' His pen stops next to one name and he grins. I peer down to see the name he's pointing at.

I nod. 'Perfect. I can't think of a better choice.'

'She's perfect,' says Mr Deery. 'I can't think of a better choice.'

Other than being a little freaked out that I apparently share a brain with my teacher, I'm stoked Mr D loves our idea.

Kathy nods. 'I *am* the perfect choice. No one knows this town better than me. Well, maybe Mr Piddles.'

'Don't gherkin worry,' Flynn explains, 'he's got a lead gherkin role too. Don't piddle in the ferret's hat. Wheeee.'

I flick through our notes. 'So, with Kathy locked in as narrator and musical tour guide, *Watterson: The Musical* is basically going to be a show about all the big events and characters of our town.'

'So I'm like Puck from *A Midsummer Night's Dream*?' says Kathy, her chest puffing out.

'Who from a what?' I have no idea what she's on about.

Kathy's looks at me like I just swore. 'Puck! Shakespeare!' She turns on Mr Deery. 'What are you teaching these kids?'

Mr Deery points at us. 'Apparently proactivity, organisation, drive, ingenuity and ambition. And saving Shakespeare for high school?'

Kathy nudges him with her shoulder. 'Touché, Mr Deery. Touché indeed!'

We haven't got time for their weird adult squabbles. I move on and get them up to speed on our progress.

'So, we've planned a rough outline of the story, chosen the main characters and picked out a bunch of songs.' I hand our redrafted lists to Mr Deery and Kathy. 'Flynn's parents are helping with the sheet music and we'll write the lyrics. Mr D, can we leave auditions up to you to organise?'

Mr D gives me a salute. 'Aye, aye, Captain. Giuseppe is putting together the set-building crew. His daughter works in construction and is pulling in some favours too. I've also spoken to Fara at Copy Cats, and they're happy to do all the promotional printing – posters, programs, etc.'

'Binita is part of the craft club at Town Hall,' adds Kathy. 'They've signed up for any costume help we might need.'

Flynn and I look at each other.

'Binita is part of a craft club?' I can't imagine her putting her phone down long enough to sew something.

Kathy shrugs. 'Apparently.'

'Don't stop judge a book by its gherkin cover, I guess. Whoop!' says Flynn.

'So that just leaves two things,' says Mr Deery. 'You two to finish writing the musical and . . . a band!'

I knew this was coming. I don't have a solution; neither does Flynn. I'm hoping Mr Deery might be able to help out.

'Yeah, I've got nothing, Mr Deery.' I point at Flynn. 'Except a pianist.'

Flynn points to the roof and then me. 'And a gherkin guitarist.'

Mr Deery nods. 'I think we need to talk to Ms Fox. She's the only one I know who can help.'

'No! I don't want her knowing about the plan. If it all fails epically, she'll be really disappointed. And still have no job.'

Mr Deery gives me his teacher look. 'I think she'll be very grateful and proud of you, regardless of the outcome. Remember, it's the effort that counts.'

Uh oh. That's the kind of thing adults say when they think you *are* going to fail. I don't just want to make 'an effort'. I want to make a difference.

'No way.' I'm not budging.

Kathy steps in. 'We don't have to tell her *why* we're doing the musical – we could just say it's one of those extra-curricular school things you teachers love making kids do.'

'Kathy!' Mr Deery glares at her. 'We don't *make* the kids do them.'

'Really?' says Kathy, and turns to me and Flynn. 'Hands up everyone who loves running around in the rain kicking a ball at eight o'clock on a Saturday morning in the middle of winter.'

We look apologetically at Mr Deery but don't raise our hands. Well, Flynn gives a little thumbs-up, but that's just a tic and we all know it doesn't count.

Kathy mimes a mic drop and smiles smugly at Mr D.

He looks to the roof and sighs. 'Fine! If we don't tell her what it's for, can we get her involved?'

'Up to gherkin you, Mac,' says Flynn.

'Sure. I guess that's fine.'

We *are* gonna need a band, after all.

'Putting on a musical is an awesome idea. I'd love to help out.'

It's no surprise that Ms Fox says yes. Like I said – best teacher ever!

'I'll combine The Ants Pants with the other school bands and some of my musician friends. A few musos I know lost their gigs at The Garage recently, so hopefully they'll be keen to join in. I'll get working on it straight away. I love it, Mac! It will be an awesome way to farewell the school.'

I catch her look. She doesn't know we know about the Arts Fiasco. They haven't made any official announcements yet, which gives me hope that there's still time to turn it around.

'You know, the end-of-year farewell, I mean,' she says nervously, trying to cover the slip-up. 'Until next year.'

She puts on a brave face but I can see the sadness in her eyes. I push the feeling of dread deep, deep down and bury it under my determination to make things right.

Ms Fox flicks through the music I handed her. 'Who wrote all this?' I point to Flynn, who's waiting outside the school gates for me. 'My friend Flynn. He's a bit of a prodigy.'

Ms Fox smiles. 'Looks like it.' She waves him over.

Flynn walks towards us slowly and I can see he's trying to hold his tics in. I've seen him do this a couple of times now and it looks a bit like he's going to sneeze and is holding his breath at the same time.

'So you're the famous Flynn?' Ms Fox says, extending her hand towards him.

'Yes. Hi,' says Flynn, and gives her some rock hands instead of shaking.

She laughs. 'I like your style,' she says, returning the rock hands. She waves the music at him. 'This is amazing, Flynn. Will you be playing with the band?'

Flynn nods.

'What instrument do you play?'

'I play the polka dot fiddle. Sorry gherkin, I don't whoop, I play piano.'

Ms Fox has that now very familiar, confused look on her face.

'I also have gherkin Tourette's wheeee!' explains Flynn.

'*Aaaaahhhh*, gotcha,' says Ms Fox, nodding. 'You got me excited for a moment. I thought we had a polka dot fiddle player for the band.'

We all laugh and I see Flynn relax. He and Ms Fox chat away about music and scores and sopranos and a whole bunch of other stuff I don't understand. I watch them, smiling. I know Mum sometimes worries that I don't have enough friends but I really do have the *best* people in my life.

ACT TWO

Scene Five

Balthazar Theatre

A montage plays out showing a progression of preparations for the musical ahead. Days tick over on a calendar as weeks pass by and the cast and crew sing.

'Theatre Nights'
(to the tune of 'Summer Nights'
from *Grease*)

Theatre lovin', we need a cast
Theatre lovin', build the set fast
Need a costume, perfect for me
Need a band, quick as can be.

Bump-in day, not far away
But uh oh those theatre nights.

Wella, wella, wella.

Help me more, help me more
'Cos my costume just ripped.
Help me more, help me more
Like do we have a script?

Uh huh, uh huh, uh huh.

I auditioned, main role for me
I auditioned, now I'm playing a tree
I built a set, it is Town Hall
Are you sure? 'Cos it looks like
the mall.

It's a mess, we must confess
But uh oh those theatre nights.

Wella, wella, wella.

Help me more, help me more
Like where is my spotlight?
Help me more, help me more
Soon it's opening night!

'That's not gonna work either!' I cross out the latest verse of Kathy's introduction song for the third time and stretch my neck. Flynn and I have been hunched over this notebook trying to figure out these lyrics for two hours now. And we are getting nowhere.

I push the book towards Flynn. 'I get what you're saying, but it's Kathy's opening song. So it has to give a sort of overview of the town, right?' The page in front of us has more words crossed out than it has written. I rub my eyes with the palms of my hands. 'Why did we leave the first song until so late? Surely that's not a smart way to do it.'

Everyone else is back at Balthazar Theatre trying to get the show up and running, but Flynn and I still haven't even finished the songs for the musical.

He picks up the pen and crosses out two more lines. 'Because whoop we knew it was going to be the gherkin hardest. Stop. And we were gherkin right.'

Although we're totally stumped on the opening number, the writing process so far has gone really well. The musical has become this sort of conveyor belt process with lots of moving parts. Flynn and I pick one of his songs, we write the lyrics, his parents help with the sheet music and then the finished product goes to Ms Fox, who starts rehearsals with the band. At the same time, Flynn records himself playing it on the piano and gives the backing track to Mr Deery so he can start rehearsals with the cast. The big problem is that we have lots of bits of a musical but still no full script. And we're running out of time. Ms Fox and Mr Deery need everything by the end of next week because the October holidays are starting and rehearsals will go into overdrive.

So Flynn and I are working on it every spare second we have.

'Let's gherkin go over the first bit again stop and see if we can figure out where to go gherkin next.' Flynn pushes the notepad back towards me and pulls his mini keyboard in front of him. He taps out the intro and I sing through what we have so far of Kathy's opening song . . .

In a very big universe, there's a fairly big planet
With a country that's all girt by sea.
To the east there's a state, and somewhere in the middle
Is a town where you might meet me!

You can find it on the map, if you Google really hard.
Its mundane facade is quite intentional
But if you look a little closer, come in, take a peek
You'll see Watterson is far from conventional.

Flynn stops playing. 'So next Kathy should gherkin take us on a bit of a stop tour to introduce the different gherkin settings we're going to whoop use. And set up the gherkin story about each. Stop.'

I scribble down the points we want to cover in the song. 'So she needs to go to Watterson Primary and we could have Tess walking down the school corridor towards her locker but then Kathy stops her before she opens it to reveal the million bucks.'

'Gherkin perfect!' says Flynn. 'She could actually whoop stop the locker from opening and gherkin say something like "We'll come back to see what's in here" wheeee.'

'Love it! Like a teaser,' I say, jotting it down. 'Then she can move to Town Hall and talk about the ex-mayor, then wander through Brennan Park and drop some hints about the infamous prank-fair.'

'Yes! It's a perfect gherkin way to set up all the whoop locations we use in the musical stop, and then she should gherkin end at her wheeee Lego house, which will be side gherkin stage. She can watch the whole gherkin show from there, popping out to narrate stop throughout the gherkin musical.'

'Okay, so how about . . .

```
Let's start right here, with our proud
Town Hall.
```

Ruled fairly by Mayor Henry Wu.

But before he was here, there was a mayor we all feared . . .

'Wu, do, you, loo. Mayor Poo in a port-a-loo!' Flynn shouts.

'Hilarious! But we better not call her Mayor Poo. Even though I totally want to. How about "But she ended up in a port-a-loo"?'

'Perfecto! Gherkin.'

I quickly write it down. I love writing songs with Flynn. I usually find last lines of a stanza really difficult. I have to change it heaps of times to match it with something that rhymes. But Flynn's tics are actually an amazing lyric generator. Writing lyrics sort of inspires his tics and they come out of him freely. I always want to be sure something is right, or works properly, before I ever try it or write it down, but all his ideas just spill out. Nothing is off limits with Flynn.

'That reminds me,' I say, flicking through my notebook a couple of pages. 'I was working on Mr Piddles's song last night. I need some help with two lines and then it's done.'

'Can gherkin do! Giraffe goes moo!'

We finish off both Kathy's and Mr Piddles's songs before bolting over to Balthazar Theatre to catch rehearsals.

We arrive a bit late to find Casey Wu yelling through a megaphone.

'Everybody, first positions!'

'STAGE MANAGER' is printed in big black letters on her t-shirt. Casey is all over the managing part.

'All right, everyone. We're doing "Kids Run the School" again, from the top.' I'm stoked we arrived in time to see this – it's one of my favourite songs. We wrote it as the intro song to Watterson Primary, and it features a guy called Aaron playing Mr Deery, Binita playing Mrs Keiren (which I just love *so* much – she's totally perfected her Mrs Keiren voice), and then Mr D roped in a bunch of kids from our class to play students. Some are here because they liked the idea of being on stage, and some because he offered bonus class credit and lollies. Good old bribery works every time!

Casey nods to Mr Deery and he counts them in. 'Five, six, seven, eight . . .'

Flynn and I hang out up the back and watch as Craig Martin and one of the younger kids sing . . .

I do my homework and what I'm told
'Cos you know I ain't no fool.
We make the teachers think they're in
charge but . . .

All the kids in the chorus join in, pumping their fist in the air.

KIDS RUN THE SCHOOL!

Tess Heckleston drags Toby to centre stage.

We found some money, we caught a crook
We thought we were pretty cool.
And we only did a short stint in
detention 'cos . . .
KIDS RUN THE SCHOOL!

The Green Peas (minus Casey, who's busy with her clipboard) are up next. Wow, Mr Deery really talked everyone into this. Zeke and Cookie sing together.

```
SRC, the school newspaper
Soon we'll have a new swimming pool
The teachers may need a coffee machine
but . . .
KIDS RUN THE SCHOOL!
```

The music slows down a little for Aaron's solo.

```
I dreamed my whole life of being a teacher
Of sharing knowledge and wisdom and smarts.
Of having kids look to me in sweet
admiration
With love and thanks in their hearts.
But I learnt very quickly . . . that's
not how it works.
At Watterson Primary you follow one rule
You pretend you're in charge and it's
under control but . . .
```

Flynn and I break into applause. I always thought that song was pretty cool, but hearing it sung by the entire chorus, with choreography, up on the stage – it's just . . . something else!

'Well, if it isn't the musical wizards themselves,' says Mr Deery, waving his hand towards us. 'For those of you who don't know, this is Mac and Flynn and they wrote this musical.'

'It's so awesome!' says Tess. 'I totally love the Funky Anchovy song. It's so 70s disco funk.'

'No way!' shouts Zeke. 'The best is "A Ninja Ain't a Ninja if You Know It". And I swear I'm not just saying that because it's about me.'

'Well, personally I like "A Heart Made of Lego",' says Kathy. 'It makes me cry every time. Although Mr Piddles likes "It Ain't Easy Being a Ferret" . . . of course!'

'I think we can agree, it's all pretty amazing,' says Mr Deery.

The doors burst open to the theatre. 'Gather round, people. Here's your schedule.'

Jennifer Heckleston waves a bunch of papers at us. 'I've been watching your rehearsals and preparation and I really think the musical's going to be a **BIG** hit, so I've extended your run to two weeks. I've bumped our performance of *The Importance of Being Earnest* so you can have access to the theatre for dress rehearsals in the lead-up.' She reaches us and starts passing out schedules. 'I'm so excited about this, everybody. Normally, we can never do musicals at Balthazar. With funding cuts, the orchestra costs and performance rights, they're just beyond our means.'

Mr Deery takes his copy of the schedule. 'Well, we appreciate you letting us use the space, Jennifer. This whole thing wouldn't be possible without it.'

She waves her hand at him and scoffs. 'That's what this place is for. Putting on shows, supporting the arts. If we can't do that, then what's the point?'

Giuseppe raises his hand. 'My daughter and her crew fixed the backstage roller door for you, Jenny. They noticed it was getting a bit stuck and thought they'd look after it while they were working on the classroom set.'

Jennifer rolls her eyes. I think she might have picked that up from her daughter, Tess. I don't know Tess *that* well, but I've still seen her do it plenty of times.

'Thank you so much, Giuseppe. I know this place is falling apart. It needs a big renovation, but that's just a pipe dream.' She looks at Flynn and I. 'Maybe when you two get Broadway famous you can remember us and throw a few bucks towards a reno?'

'Consider it gherkin done!' agrees Flynn. He obviously has a lot more confidence in our future success than I do.

'Can someone get the door?' Toby's mum Fara is trying to push the theatre doors open with her butt and squeeze a trolley through at the same time. Tess and Toby run to grab the doors and Fara barrels on through. 'All right, you toe-tapping, triple-threat theatre types, the posters are in.' She drives the trolley down the aisle like it's a dodgem car, kids leaping into the seats to save their toes from being flattened. Coming to a screeching halt, she grabs hold of a cardboard tube, yanking a rolled-up poster out of it. 'TADA!!!' she booms, holding up her handiwork for all to see.

'Wow!' A collective gasp comes from everyone in the theatre.

And wow is right. It looks like a legit Broadway poster. Big gold letters across the top read, '*Watterson: The Musical*'. A silhouette of the town hall fills up the centre of the poster, casting a shadow across the bottom half of the page, which creates a map of Brennan Park. Popping up from the park are a Lego house, a park bench and a giant grey ironbark tree. Hanging from the branches of the tree are money notes, which fly away into a treasure chest. A long shadow of a man sneaking with a bag of money leans away from the box. There are guinea pigs and Mr Piddles and a crowd of kids with their fists in the air. The poster is packed with little Watterson-isms. The more you look, the more you see.

'It's amazing,' I say. 'You've managed to get everything in there.'

Fara beams proudly. 'Well, everything here makes Watterson the place it is. Couldn't bear to leave anyone, or anything, out. The town wouldn't be the same without any of it.'

She's right. Just like Watterson Primary wouldn't be the same without Ms Fox. Staring at this poster fills me with confidence – the Arts Fiasco will NOT go ahead.

'And gherkin look!' Flynn points to the writing at the bottom of the poster.

My eyes scan down to read the curly font. A lump forms in my throat and my eyes well up just a little.

'Lyrics by Mac Cooper, music by Flynn Vanderberg,' I whisper.

Flynn gives my shoulder a squeeze. 'Pretty gherkin cool, huh?'

'I . . . it's . . .'

Kathy laughs. 'That's the spirit, Mac, keep those words saved up for the musical. Well done, kids, what a huge achievement.'

'This is gherkin going straight on the stop poster wall,' Flynn announces with a grin. 'Mum and Dad are gonna be so gherkin jealous whoop!'

'Absolutely,' agrees Mr Deery. 'And your mum must be so proud too, Mac.'

I swallow. 'Sure is.'

The truth is, I haven't told Mum about any of this. She knows I've been spending all my time with Flynn and 'the new group', and that we're rehearsing for an end-of-year show. But I haven't exactly specifically mentioned it's actually a musical. I haven't found the right moment. Turns out I'm *very* good at being vague.

I mean, how do I tell her that I'm leaving my rock roots behind? With everything that's going on with her job, I haven't had the guts to break it to her that I've unintentionally turned my rock band into a musical theatre orchestra, have become part of a Broadway-composing duo and spend all my spare time rehearsing for a musical theatre production she knows nothing about. It seems like a *lot* for her to hear at once, so I'm just . . . taking my time.

'This is really great, thanks, Fara.' I take the poster from her and roll it up, sliding it back into the cylinder.

I mean I'm not actually lying to Mum. She knows Flynn and I are working on music together and that I'm spending a lot of time at rehearsals.

She knows where I'm at all the time, and with who. I've just skipped over the specifics. She has enough on her plate at the moment.

That, and I'm scared to break her heart.

Fara hands me a box. 'Eccellente! There's proofs of the program and leaflets in there too. Double-check everything and let me know when they're approved and we'll start the print run.'

'Thanks so much, Fara, it all looks amazing.'

'You're very welcome. Okay, gotta run, more deliveries to do. Later!'

I wave goodbye as she zooms back up the aisle, then pass our latest work to Mr Deery. 'Here's the new stuff, Mr D. We've only got one song to go – the grand finale. Have you spoken to Ms Fox?'

'Sure have,' says Mr Deery. 'We start rehearsals with the band next week. Then it will be back-to-back practice during the holidays. You kids ready to work?'

'You bet!' we all yell.

'Okay, we'll leave you gherkin to it,' says Flynn, grabbing my arm. 'We've got stop somewhere we have to gherkin be.' He waves his mobile phone at Mr Deery. 'Call if you gherkin need anything wheeee.'

Mr Deery nods and Flynn drags me out of the theatre.

'Where do we have to be?' I ask as we exit into the foyer.

Flynn spins me around and grins at me. 'I have a little gherkin surprise for you.'

'What?'

'So it seemed gherkin ridiculous to me that you've whoop **NEVER** seen a stop live musical. So, the Vanderberg wheeee family got you a little gherkin present.'

Flynn pulls four tickets out of his pocket and waves them in my face. 'Guess who's gherkin going to see stop *Matilda the* gherkin *Musical* in the whoop city tonight! Tadpoles have rights too!'

My eyeballs suddenly feel too big for their sockets as I try to focus on the bits of printed cardboard dancing in front of my face. I snatch them out of Flynn's hands. He's not lying. Four tickets to *Matilda*. For tonight! I run my thumb over the raised print. A real live musical. In a theatre. I can't even.

Flynn hops on the spot, his arm flinging up and giving me a peace sign, thumbs-up, rock hands – the entire menu of his hand tics. 'Sooooo gherkin, what do you stop say?'

I give a small squeal and fling my arms around him. 'I say you are the best gherkin friend EVER!"

'Ha! I'll stop take that as a gherkin compliment. Whoop!'

I don't think I've ever gotten from Balthazar Theatre to home so fast. Dodging bike riders, ducking around slow walkers, leaping small children in a single bound. I'm probably just a blur to the people I overtake on the street as the wind rushes past them.

I burst through the front door. 'Muuuuuuuum!'

'Buuuuuuuum!' replies Stevie from the lounge room. I run in to see him sitting on the floor, halfway through building what looks like a toilet out of Lego. It's actually pretty impressive, but I don't have time to be impressed right now.

'Is Mum here?'

‘Here is the world’s biggest toilet!’ he says, climbing a Lego minifigure up the rim of the toilet seat. ‘Now there’s no way he can miss!’ Stevie cracks himself up.

‘Stevie!’

Without looking up, he points down the hall. ‘Bedroom. Getting ready for work, shmirk.’

I push through the bedroom door. Mum’s pulling on a yet another Fleetwood Mac t-shirt (surprise, surprise). She looks tired, but still manages a smile.

‘Heya, Mac, how was practice?’

‘Fine. Good. Doesn’t matter. Mum, guess what? Flynn got us tickets to a show tonight in the city. Can I go? Can I?’

Mum frowns as she half attempts to fix her hair a bit. ‘I haven’t even met Flynn yet. Or his parents. And we can’t afford tickets to shows right now, sorry, Mac.’

I shake my head. ‘No, it’s fine. They’re comps. Like free tickets. And here.’ I shove a piece of paper into Mum’s hand. ‘Flynn said to call his parents, no problem. Please, Mum, c’mon, I never get to do stuff like this.’

She looks at me, a little offended. 'What are you talking about? I take you to see bands play at The Garage all the time.'

I swallow. 'Um, yeah, I know. But this is a big show, in the city. Please, Mum.'

She puts her hands on her hips. 'Who's playing?'

'Huh?'

'Which band?'

I pause. This is it. This is where I tell her I'm going to see a musical. It's perfect timing, because it's not even my choice, right? I can blame it on Flynn's family. Say that *they* are really into musicals and I'm just being dragged along. I open my mouth to say all of this . . .

'They're called The Matildas.'

What is wrong with me? Just say it, Mac. Three words. It's . . . a . . . musical.

Mum scrunches up her nose. 'The Matildas? Never heard of them.'

'Um, they're a pretty new rock band,' I explain. 'Up and comers, you know.'

She smiles and nods. 'Nice one, supporting the indies, Mac, I like it.' She pauses and then smiles.

'Let me call Flynn's parents, and then why not. I'm sure Mrs Moshie can handle Stevie on her own. Well, I hope, anyway.'

She gives me a kiss on the head, grabs her phone and punches in the number on the piece of paper.

I hover just outside the door. Why did I even bother lying? She's gonna find out straight away from Flynn's mum that we're going to a musical. Maybe she won't even care . . . I look at the twenty or so rock band t-shirts crammed into her wardrobe. The posters of Fleetwood Mac covering her bedroom walls. The signed album framed above her bed. Who am I kidding? She'll never understand. This is not going to go down well.

I listen in to her half of the conversation.

'Hi, it's Nikki Cooper, Mac's mum . . . yes, same here . . . I know . . . yeah, it's really great, isn't it?'

I lean in closer, but there's no way I can hear what Remy's saying.

'Are you sure it's okay? . . . of course he'd love to . . . oh, okay . . . yes . . . oh, really . . . right . . . okay . . . uh huh.'

Mum's tone has changed. I can hear it in her voice. I know for sure Remy has broken the news to her. My heart pounds against my ribs like a bass drum. This is it. Mum's going to be so disappointed in me. I've crushed her dreams. Her son will never be a rock star.

'No, I understand. Of course . . . well, if you're sure it's okay . . . thank you so much . . . yeah, for sure . . . bye.'

I wait a beat, holding my breath.

'Mac!'

I exhale and round the corner with my head down.

'Why didn't you tell me?' Mum asks.

I can't look at her. I just shrug. 'I didn't think you'd understand.'

'Well, you could help me understand. Do you really think I'm that narrow-minded that I can't understand people who are different to me?'

I take a deep breath. She's talking like I'm a different species just because I love Broadway.

'Well, Mum, sometimes you can be a bit sort of, I dunno, snobby about different types of . . .'

'Mac! Do you really think that? Do you really think I would have a problem with your best friend just because he has Tourette's?'

I look up. 'Huh?'

'I'm so happy you've found a friend you get along with so well, Mac. But you should have told me.'

'Told you that Flynn has Tourette's?'

'Yes.'

'Why?'

'Because . . . because . . . well, I should know these things.'

I'm so confused. Why are we talking about Flynn's Tourette's when I should be getting yelled at for wanting to see a musical? Does she not know?

'Okaaaaay,' I say. 'Ah, Flynn has Tourette's. Now, can I go tonight?'

'Of course you can.' Mum rubs her hands together and looks around the room. I can see she wants to say something.

'Do you have any questions, Mum? The more you ask, the more you learn.' I'm sure Flynn won't mind me quoting him.

Mum looks nervous. 'Does he . . . does he swear a lot?'

I laugh out loud. Mum doesn't see the joke. But unless she's offended by the word gherkin, I don't think she has to worry.

'You've been watching too much TV, Mum. Less than ten per cent of people with Tourette's have coprolalia.'

Mum looks at me like I'm speaking another language.

I put my hand on hers. 'It's the actual name for the swearing tic. Flynn doesn't have it. And even if he did, so what? It doesn't mean I'm gonna suddenly start swearing. Flynn's the best, Mum. You're gonna love him.'

Mum smiles at me. 'I bet I will. You kids have fun tonight, okay?'

I jump up and down a little. 'So I can go?'

She nods. 'You can go.'

I give her a massive squeeze and bolt to my bedroom to get ready.

As I get out of the shower, I'm buzzing. My first real live musical . . . and it's in the city! We hardly ever go to the city. I'm bouncing so much I can barely wrap my towel around myself. Opening the bathroom door, I exit in a cloud of steam.

Very dramatic. Mum's just hanging up the phone and turns to me as I walk out.

'I'm so sorry, Mac,' she says.

'Sorry for what?' Nothing can bring me down right now.

'Mrs Moshie is sick and can't come tonight. You're going to have to stay home and watch Stevie.'

Nothing except that.

'But Muuuuuuuuuum.'

'I'm sorry, Mac, but I can't miss a shift. I hardly ever ask you to do this.'

It's true, she doesn't. Despite having to work nights, Mum tries really hard to make sure I don't have to be the parent. Although most times, I really don't mind it. But not tonight.

'Please, Mum.'

'I'm sorry, Mac, I really am. But you're going to have to call Flynn.' She picks up my phone from the kitchen table and passes it to me. Mum and I have always been super close – I almost never get angry with her. But right now, I just wanna cry. I snatch the phone from her hand and dial Flynn's number.

'What's gherkin up, Mac? Excited for stop tonight?'

'I can't come.'

'What? Wheeee. Why not?'

'The babysitter can't come and I gotta look after Stevie.'

'Nooooo!'

I don't even know what to say. I feel a bit like that time I got an accidental soccer ball to the gut from Anishka Batan. Kinda sick and hurt at the same time.

'Hang on a gherkin sec. Whoop!' I hear Flynn put the phone down and some talking in the background. In a few minutes, he comes back.

'Problem gherkin solved. Dad reckons he can stop get an extra whoop ticket. Stevie can come too. Gherkin. And you can both wheeee stay at our place tonight if you want. See you at five gherkin thirty. Whoop.'

Without waiting for an answer, he hangs up. I turn to Mum, who's looking all kinds of guilty.

'I really am sorry, Mac.'

I give her a small smile. 'Don't be sorry yet. They can get an extra ticket. Can Stevie come too?'

'Where am I coming?' Stevie's head pops around the kitchen door.

'You wanna come with me and Flynn to see a show?'

His eyes narrow. 'What kind of show?'

I pause.

Mum folds her arms. 'Isn't he a bit young to be going to see a band?'

'Am not!' says Stevie. Not because he wants to see a band, but just because he hates being told he's too young for anything.

'Not at all,' I say. 'It's a show for kids. That's the whole point.'

Mum looks at her watch and freaks out. 'I'm going to be late for work.'

'But can we go?' I ask.

She looks at Stevie. 'Do you want to go to a music show with Mac and Flynn?'

Stevie nods.

'Will you be good?'

He nods again.

She turns to me. 'Are you sure it's gonna be okay for a five-year-old? You know what a nightmare he is when he gets bored.'

I nod.

'Fine!' She starts to run around the house, grabbing her stuff. 'Text me when they pick you up. And text me again when you get there. *And* when you leave.'

I follow her around as she grabs a jacket and her bag.

'Flynn said we can stay at his place if you want?'

Mum searches around for something. 'Both of you go back to his place. Call me when you get back.' She throws things off the table. 'If I don't finish too late, I'll pick you up on the way home. WHERE ARE MY KEYS?'

I grab them from next to the microwave and pass them to her. She smiles, snatching them from me. 'What would I do without you? Stevie, here, now.'

Stevie comes in and stands next to me. Mum looks us both in the eyes. 'Stay together. Be good. Use your manners. And what's most important?'

'Don't let Stevie out of my sight,' I recite.

Mum shakes her head. 'No. Have fun and rock on!' She gives us rock hands and we give them back, Stevie adding a little tongue-out action for effect. Mum kisses us each and heads for the door.

Just as she's about to disappear, I yell to her.

'Mum!'

She spins around. 'Yeah?'

'Thanks,' I say. 'I love you.'

She smiles. 'Love you too, kiddo. Have fun.'

And with that, the best mum in the whole wide universe disappears through the door.

I turn to face Stevie.

'Now let's get you cleaned up and ready for a show.'

'What's wrong with what I'm wearing?' Stevie asks, looking down at his outfit.

'You're not wearing any pants, for starters,' I point out.

He shrugs. 'So?'

'This is NOT a pants optional event!' I grab his arm and drag him to the bedroom to change.

ACT TWO

Scene Six

Empire Theatre

Mac walks into the Empire Theatre. It's like nothing he's ever seen before. The roof stretches into the sky and people are dressed in suits and sparkles. A woman selling programs stands on a tiny podium in the centre of the foyer and wine glasses make soft 'tinks' as people cheers and laugh.

'A Touch of the Fancy'

(to the tune of 'A Spoonful of Sugar'
from *Mary Poppins*)

In every show that you will see
There's just a touch of la-da-dee
You don a hat and snap!
The show's a SHOW!

And every person to be seen
Looks a little like the Queen.
An act! A play! There's just one way to say . . . that
A touch of the fancy helps the theatre to shine
The theatre to shi-ine
Theatre to shine.
Just a touch of the fancy helps the theatre to shine
In a most expected way!

'Mac! Have a look at this.' Flynn's dad, Levi, calls me over to check out the program he's holding. He flicks through to find a photo of the actor who plays Mrs Wormwood and points to her. 'That's my friend Davina. She's the one who got us the tickets.'

Stevie tries to look too, but he's not tall enough to see over the program in Levi's hands.

I slowly take in all the photos on the page then stop, thrusting my finger at one of them. 'Wait! Is that Kay Angelos?'

Levi nods. 'Yeah, you know her?'

'Know her? Doesn't everyone know Kay Angelos?'

He laughs. 'Well, everyone in musical theatre certainly does. You really do know your stuff, Mac. She plays Miss Honey.'

I can't believe I'm going to see my very first live musical AND it's going to star Kay Angelos. This night could not get any better.

Stevie tries to walk away towards a giant cut-out of Matilda, but I squeeze his hand and yank him back to my side. I just need him to be Perfect Stevie for one night. Just tonight.

'Do you think, maybe, we could get to meet her?' I ask.

Levi shuts the program. 'I don't know, Mac. Usually I like to go and say hi to Davina backstage after the show, but it takes them so long to get changed and come out and we'll probably have to leave straight away. I don't want to get you kids home too late. I'm sorry.'

'Oh, that's totally fine. I'm just so excited to see her on stage.' I reach for the program. 'Could I please have a look at that?'

Levi passes it to me. 'That's yours to keep.'

'Really?' I ask, running my fingers over the emboss on the front.

'Sure, we'll just get another one.'

'What about me?' Stevie pipes up.

'We can share,' I growl at him through gritted teeth. He probably thinks the programs are free, but my tone of voice will let him know one copy is enough for both of us. He gets the message straight away and pulls his head back in.

'Can we whoop get some gherkin popcorn please, Dad? Stop.'

Flynn's already dragging his dad to the snack bar without waiting for a response, leaving Stevie and me with his mum.

'I've been meaning to thank you, Mac,' says Remy.

'Me? What for?'

'For being there for Flynn the other day after he had that run-in.'

I grit my teeth. 'Oh, you mean with the butt-face jerk-bag?'

Remy laughs. 'That's the one. It means a lot to us knowing that Flynn has someone like you. You're a wonderful friend, Mac.'

I feel myself blush and focus on my suddenly-very-interesting feet. 'Nah, Flynn's the awesome friend.'

Stevie tugs on Remy's jacket. 'I'm a good friend too.'

'I have no doubt,' she says, turning her attention to Stevie and giving my cheeks a chance to cool down. 'So have you two been to the theatre before?' Remy is wearing a purple jacket that's made of velvet or something and Stevie won't stop patting her. It's so embarrassing. I snatch his hand away.

'No, this is our first time,' I say, trying to use my best manners to make up for the fact that my little brother thinks she's a goat at the petting zoo.

'Oh, you're going to love it. *Matilda* is amazing.'

'Amazing Spiderman,' says Stevie, reaching for the coat again. I grab his hand and hold it, even when he tries to tug away.

'What was that about Spiderman?' she asks.

'Sorry, it's a thing he does where he takes the last word you say and makes something else out of it. We're hoping he'll grow out of it.'

She smiles at Stevie. 'Well, I hope not. It sounds like a fun improv exercise to me. How about . . . my coat feels like a snuggly bear!'

'Bare bums in the bath!'

I cringe. Does he have to be so embarrassing? But apparently Remy finds him hilarious. She crouches down and continues to play his word games. He pats her coat as they talk and she doesn't seem to mind in the slightest. Remy laughs as Stevie tells her how I made him change his pants four times before we came but I let him wear his favourite bowtie. I relax a little. Remy clearly doesn't care that Stevie asks a million questions or squeals too loud when he sees choc tops or scratches his butt in public. So maybe I shouldn't care so much either. This is Stevie's night too. It's okay if he's only Almost-Perfect Stevie. I let go of his hand and wander off to explore the foyer.

A trailer for the musical plays on a big screen above the bar. Kids in school uniforms jump and sing, running across the stage, dancing in unison and climbing on the set. How do these kids get parts in a musical?! Do their parents just let them miss school for this? Do they get paid? I never thought in a million years I'd ever be able to work in musical theatre, but here's a bunch of kids doing it already . . . and they can't be much older than me.

A hand grabs my shoulder. 'That'll be gherkin us one day. Whoop!' Flynn stands next to me, staring up at the big screen.

'You really think so?'

He grins. 'We're already whoop well on our gherkin way. Bet none of those gherkin kids have written their own stop musical. Wheeee!'

He's right. We've done something big. Something to be proud of.

A bell rings throughout the foyer and Flynn grabs my arm. 'Gherkin showtime! Hurry up, hedgehog.'

An usher leads us to our seats and we settle into the cushy red velvet chairs. Stevie bounces around on his.

I death-stare him into stopping. 'What did I say about sitting in a theatre?' I whisper to him.

'Bums on seats till the end,' he recites back to me. 'But you never said no bouncing.'

'And *no bouncing*!' I say through gritted teeth.

'You gherkin excited, Stevie?' Flynn asks.

'I'm SO gherkin excited, Flynn!' Stevie says, bouncing again.

'Stop that!' I say, pushing down on his thigh.

'You're no gherkin fun,' says Stevie.

'Stop that too!'

'But he says it,' Stevie points at Flynn.

I drag his hand down. 'You know it's because of his Tourette's. We talked about this.'

'Yeah, it's stop kinda my gherkin thing,' Flynn says gently. 'Maybe you could whoop find your own gherkin word, Stevie.'

Stevie sulks. 'But I really like gherkin.'

The lights lower and a hush falls over the audience.

'Whoop! Gherkin.' Flynn reaches into his bag and pulls out something that looks like a rubber mat. He unrolls it across his lap. 'Wheeee!'

I look at the mat on Flynn's lap. It's a rubber keyboard. 'What's that for?' I ask.

'Whoop! I use it to stop play along with the musical. It helps me focus on the gherkin show.'

I nod. 'Does it help keep the tics quiet?'

Flynn shakes his head at me. 'You gotta let gherkin go of your stuffy ideas about stop theatre. It's not whoop all about sitting still and being gherkin quiet. Music is noise wheeee. Music is passion. Music is a gherkin celebration, Mac. And none of those things are stop quiet. Sound the ZOMBIE ALARMS!'

That last tic was really loud. I look around but no one's staring. Not like at Patty's Burger Barn.

Flynn grins at me. 'You can chillax gherkin. This is a whoop relaxed theatre performance.'

'A what?' I whisper.

A spotlight illuminates the stage and there stands Kay Angelos. THE Kay Angelos! She lifts a microphone to her mouth.

'We welcome you to tonight's *relaxed* performance of *Matilda*. That means if you'd like to make noise, wiggle around or even pop out for a break then you are very welcome to do so.' Kay points to a row of red lights above the stage. 'The red lights up there will blink a minute before any particularly loud noises. We hope you all enjoy this relaxed performance and, if you ask me, you all made an excellent decision.' Kay winks at the audience. 'The uptight performances are nowhere near as fun!'

'A relaxed performance?' I ask.

'Yeah stop,' says Flynn. 'Theatre without all the judge-y gherkin stares. It's whoop awesome!'

Stevie turns to me. 'Does that mean I can bounce on my seat?'

'No! Well . . . maybe.' I look at Flynn. 'Does it?'

Flynn just laughs at me. 'Relax, Mac. Enjoy the gherkin show.'

The music starts and Flynn taps away softly on his rubber piano. One day it's totally going to be him in that orchestra pit, I just know it. Stevie leans towards me.

'What's this show even about?' he asks.

I turn his head back to face the stage. 'Watch and find out.'

The curtains open wide and so does Stevie's mouth. For the next few hours Stevie is enthralled. He's so excited by the dancing and the singing and the energy that explodes off the stage that he bounces around on his seat non-stop. And I let him.

In the car ride home, Flynn and Stevie are playing some kind of spontaneous storytelling game that combines Stevie's word thing and Flynn's tics. I've given up trying to tell Stevie to stop copying Flynn for a few reasons: Flynn will have no problem telling Stevie if he crosses the line; Stevie copies everyone he admires, so really it's kind of a compliment (and at least I'll get a break from Bandit's catchcry, 'cheese and crackers') and, finally, I just want to play the last three hours over and over in my head so I don't forget one minute of it.

The lyrics, the music, the way the voices joined together and filled the theatre almost making me rise up out of my seat. The lights and the set and how every single person in the audience, young and old, hung off every word sung and was along for the ride.

My hands are still tingling and sore from clapping as loud as I possibly could, for as long as I possibly could at the end – and I still don't feel like I showed the cast and crew enough appreciation. I smile, remembering that Stevie was clapping just as hard, his eyes wide, standing on his tippy-toes trying to see the stage over the standing ovation.

'Hey, Mac,' says Remy, snapping me out of my daydream. She passes her program over her shoulder to me in the back seat. 'Let's switch programs.'

'Um, okay,' I say, passing her mine. 'Why?'

Remy turns over her shoulder. 'I think you're going to like this one better.' She gives me a wink and turns back to face the front.

I flick through the program and there, below the photo of Kay Angelos, is something scrawled in black Sharpie.

Thanks for coming to see the show, Mac. May all your musical dreams come true. Kay Angelos.

Turns out this night *can* get better. I hug the program to my chest as I watch the lights of the city speed by. I have never felt quite like this before – quite so sure of what I want to do. This feeling inside me right now, this is what music can do. This is why our musical has to be a huge success, why we have to save Ms Fox's job and the Watterson arts program, and end this Arts Fiasco. Because without music, life is just blah!

Mum swung by on her way home from work to pick up Stevie but said I could stay at Flynn's. I lie in a makeshift bed on his floor, staring up at his roof while Flynn tics in his bed next to me. His mum offered for me to sleep in the lounge 'cos Flynn's tics might keep me awake but I find them kind of rhythmic and soothing.

'So did you gherkin like it?' Flynn asked.

'It was the most amazing thing I've ever seen in my whole life.'

'So are you stop gonna tell your gherkin mum that we're writing a gherkin musical now? Whoop.'

I smile at the roof. 'I am.'

'Good. Wheeee.'

I prop myself up on my elbow. 'Is it hard to get to sleep? With the tics?'

'Yeah, sometimes. Stop, whoop. Music helps me gherkin. Do you stop mind if I whoop put on my gherkin headphones?'

I lie back down. 'I'd like it even more if you played it out loud.'

I hear the soft beep as Flynn connects to his Bluetooth speaker. He flicks through a playlist and then *The Lion King* musical plays softly through the room.

'I hope you don't gherkin mind, but I find Mufasa good to whoop fall asleep to.'

'Sounds perfect to me.'

'Hey, Mac? Stop.'

'Yeah, Flynn?'

'Our musical is gonna gherkin be a huge success. Whoop. You gherkin know that, right?'

'I do, Flynn. I actually do.'

I close my eyes and let 'The Circle of Life' put me to sleep.

ACT TWO

Scene Seven

The Streets of Watterson

Mac and Flynn walk towards Balthazar Theatre. Their walk has a new bounce in it. They look confident and excited. Ready to see how their show is progressing, they link arms and skip down the road.

'We're off to See Rehearsal'

(to the tune of 'We're off to See the Wizard' from *The Wizard of Oz*)

We're off to see rehearsal
The awesome rehearsal of ours.
We hear it is, the best in the biz
If we do say so ourselves.
If ever a perfect rehearsal there was
Then ours must be the one because
Because, because, because, because, because
We don't have a reason so let's just say 'cos.

We're off to see rehearsal
The awesome rehearsal of ours.

'What is that smell?' I wrap my hands over my nose *and* mouth to stop both the smell and the threat of my breakfast reappearing.

Flynn looks at me and shrugs.

It's bad. Like, really bad. Like, back when I used to help change Stevie's nappies kind of bad. Flynn and I pull our t-shirts over our noses and speed up our walk.

Today is the first big rehearsal for the show. Everyone has been working separately, perfecting their parts until now, but today we get to see it all – cast, band, set, costumes. It's going to be amazing to see all the hard work that's been put in so far pull together on stage.

But what we see as we round the corner to Balthazar Theatre is not the scene I imagined. Instead of an excited buzz of people trying on costumes and the band warming up inside the theatre, the entire cast and crew of our musical is gathered outside. Musicians sit propped on their instrument cases, kids group cross-legged in the carpark, vans carrying costumes sit half unpacked. Everyone is covering their noses.

You can't miss the smell.

Flynn and I take our walk to a run. Mr Deery, Giuseppe, Binita and Kathy are huddled in a group at the front.

'What's going on, Mr D?' I ask, coming to a halt in front of them.

The look on Mr Deery's face tells me it's not good news.

'Apparently there's a little problem with the sewage pipe in the theatre. We're just waiting to hear from Jennifer.'

'Little problem?' yells Giuseppe. 'It smells like an entire heard of cattle did their business in the foyer. I've heard critics says "the theatre stinks" but this is a whole new level.'

'How gherkin are we gherkin, whoop going to rehearse stop? Poo river floods the *Titanic*!' asks Flynn.

Kathy passes Mr Piddles to Flynn. The ferret curls up in the crook of his elbow as Flynn strokes his back.

'Let's just take it one step at a time,' says Kathy. 'Jenny will be out in a sec and we can find out what's going on.'

Binita looks at her watch. 'She said "ten minutes" twenty minutes ago. Can't you go and find out, Kathy?'

Kathy salutes Binita. 'Aye, aye, Captain Impatience! Can Mr Piddles stay with you, Flynn?'

Flynn nods and Kathy heads towards the theatre.

'What happened?' I ask Mr Deery.

'Apparently they've been having some issues with the bathrooms, but something big broke overnight. Jenny's not sure what the damage is yet.'

Giuseppe coughs and covers his mouth. 'Well, the damage to my senses is real. How long are we going to hang around this poop-fest for?'

Before Mr D can answer, Kathy comes back with Jennifer. One whiff of Tess's mum tells us the smell is *much* worse inside.

'I'm sorry, everyone,' she says, shaking her head. 'The sewage pipe has exploded and the entire place is flooded. There's no way you can get in there today. Or anytime soon. I'm going to have to cancel all rehearsals and shows until I can get someone in here to take a look.'

Mr Deery nods his head. 'We understand, Jenny. Thanks.'

'Sorry,' Jennifer says again. 'Sorry, everyone.' She runs back inside.

'What are we going to do now?' I ask.

Mr Deery looks at Giuseppe, Giuseppe looks at Kathy and Kathy looks at Binita, but Binita has already walked off, talking into her phone.

'Could we go to the gherkin school, Mr Deery?' Flynn suggests. 'Rehearse in the stop hall gherkin?'

Mr Deery shakes his head. 'I'll never get hold of Mrs Keiren on a Sunday, and those things have to be organised weeks in advance.'

'What about the Watto Mall carpark?' I say.

'There's no way they'll close it off to shoppers,' Kathy says. 'They like the money too much.'

'Town Hall, maybe?' Mr Deery offers.

'It's Sunday,' says Giuseppe. 'There's bingo, bridge AND line dancing today. We've got no chance of getting in.'

Mr Deery sighs. 'Maybe we'll just have to cancel.'

'But everyone's already here,' I plead.

Flynn nods. 'Yeah, it would be really bad gherkin luck to cancel our first whoop full run-through.'

Binita strides back into the group. 'I've got us a space,' she announces, snapping the cover of her phone shut. 'Only for today. It's the pet food warehouse on the next corner, so I can't promise the smell will be that much better, but it's big, and it's empty until tomorrow, so it will do.'

We all stare at her.

'That's amazing, Binita,' I say. 'Thank you.'

'It's no big deal,' she says, patting down her hair. 'I want to sing today and no amount of sewage is going to stop me. Now, what are you all waiting for? Let's move this rehearsal down the road. Harry will meet us there with the keys. Come on.' She claps her hands impatiently, herding us like farm animals. 'Move it!'

Before we know it, the rehearsal is in full swing. Mr Dinesh and his art director, Cookie, are adding the finishing touches to their incredibly realistic sets, Ms Fox's orchestra – the school band combined with her adult muso friends – sound amazing, the cast is trying on costumes between scenes, props are being handed out and labelled for return and Mr Deery is running the whole thing like he runs his classroom – wonderfully organised chaos!

Everyone's doing something. Kids who aren't on stage are helping with painting and cutting, parents and teachers are setting up a snack table for lunch and the warehouse is buzzing with excitement.

The Funky Anchovy scene has just ended and Kathy is doing her solo as she leads the audience down the 'road' to the set of Balthazar Theatre, where the 'Scotty gets caught' scene takes place and one of my favourite songs, 'Just Hanging in His Boxers', will be sung.

Mr Deery's on his phone, pacing back and forth, as Kathy finishes her song. He hangs up and then calls into the megaphone. 'Great job, Kathy. Right, can we get all the kids on stage for the boxers song? We haven't rehearsed the choreography for this yet, so Ms Fox are you happy to just run through with the band and singing so we can make sure that's all down? And then Ms Jensen will work on the dance while the rest of us jump back to "Scribble Scrabble Squabble" with Giuseppe and his crew.'

'Roger that!' says Ms Fox, clapping her hands and ushering the kids onto the area marked out as 'stage.' 'Just gather here for now and let's take it from the top.'

That taken care of, Mr Deery walks over to us. 'Bad news, kids. Jenny just called. She's got a plumber and a builder at the theatre now. There's major structural damage. They have to close the theatre down.'

'For how long?!' I ask.

'Indefinitely. It's going to cost a lot to fix, and Jenny says they just don't have those kinds of funds available.'

'But where are we gherkin going to do the stop show?' asks Flynn.

Mr Deery rubs the back of his neck. 'I don't know.'

That answer's not good enough. 'We have to find somewhere.' I throw my arm out towards all the people working around us. 'Too many people have put in too much hard work to pull the pin now.' My own disappointment is one thing, but there's no way I can let all these people down.

'Binita whoop!' Flynn waves her over.

She taps on her phone as she heads towards us. How does she not trip over stuff all the time? She never looks where she's going.

Without looking up – 'What?'

'The theatre is gherkin out. Could we stop use this place for the gherkin show?'

She shakes her head. 'This is a one-off. *Maaaaaaybe* we could get it for another rehearsal or two, but there's no way Harry will let us do a bunch of shows in here with an audience and everything. No way!'

'What are we going to do?' I ask nobody in particular.

Mr Deery puts his hand on my arm. 'We'll figure something out, Mac. We've got a few weeks to come up with an alternative solution. In the meantime, we keep rehearsing wherever we can. We'll figure it out.'

I don't share his confidence.

'Mr Deery!' yells Ms Fox. 'Can you come here for a sec?'

Mr D gives my arm a squeeze then goes to help Ms Fox.

I feel defeated. Last night I was so sure of everything, so filled with confidence, and now, thanks to a tidal wave of toilet water, I feel like we're back to square one.

'I'm going for a walk,' I tell Flynn. 'I need to think.'

'Want me to gherkin come?'

I shake my head. 'I'll be back soon.'

I duck out of the warehouse and stand on the footpath, looking around. I cross the street and cut behind the town hall to Brennan Park.

There aren't many people around, so I take a seat on a bench under a huge tree and try to think. Mr Deery's right, we've put too much work into the musical to just give up, but where could we possibly hold a show now that Balthazar Theatre has become a giant toilet? It's not like Watterson has two theatres. The town hall community space isn't big enough to fit the show *and* the audience. The school hall won't work either. It gets used every day so we'd have to pack everything up after each show. Plus Mrs Keiren clearly isn't very interested in the arts.

I look around the park. This is where it all started; my love of Broadway. Three years ago, when Watterson was trying to be all hip by having an outdoor cinema – its first and last. I stare at the spot over near the drinking fountain where Mum had set up our picnic rug that night. The night that changed my life.

'Okay, that's everything,' said Mum, dumping the last load of stuff on the picnic blanket. It was a few days after Stevie's third birthday and he'd already found his way into the esky and was tucking into the leftover cake.

We were surrounded by food and chairs and blankets and toys. Anyone would think we were camping out for a week. 'Mum, do you *really* think we need all this stuff?'

'Well, I don't know what you're supposed to bring to an outdoor cinema,' she said. 'So I just brought everything.'

We had gotten there early to make sure we nabbed a good spot and lucky we did, because Brennan Park was filling up fast. Mum brought a folding chair for Mrs Moshie and, even though she was just settling in two seconds ago, she was already fast asleep. Stevie was in his Peppa Pig pyjamas and Mum was hoping that he'd fall asleep soon too.

She looked at her phone. 'Okay, two hours till the movie starts. What do you want to do until then?'

I shrugged. 'The kids at school said they play another movie before the main one, like a freebie for the people who come early.'

Mum knelt down and pulled Stevie's cream-covered fingers out of the cake, snapping the plastic lid shut. 'I don't know if I can sit through two movies.' She whipped out a baby wipe and started cleaning Stevie up. 'What is it?'

'Don't know.' I pulled a blanket up over me, opened a packet of Twisties and nestled into my beanbag, staring at the stars starting to appear overhead. Mrs Moshie snored softly in the chair next to me.

The giant screen at the front of the park flickered to life and a driving beat pumped through the surrounding speakers. I could feel the rhythm in my chest as a camera zoomed through the streets and into a bedroom, where a girl was getting ready. I sat up straight in my beanbag, eyes glued to the screen. A can, a shake, a spray and in sparkling blue letters across the screen – 'HAIRSPRAY'.

'You're kidding me!' said Mum. 'No way I'm sitting through two hours of this cheese-ball stuff.'

But I barely heard her as Tracy Turnblad sang to me, spinning through her house. 'What is it?' I asked, unable to tear my eyes away.

'One of those corny musicals.' Mum swept Stevie up in her arms. 'I'm going to take Stevie to the playground for a bit, then maybe go get us a pizza from The Funky Anchovy. You coming?'

Tracy was now out on the streets singing to everybody who passed by. The hair, the costumes, the music – I didn't want to miss a second of it.

'Ah, nah, Mum, I'd better stay with Mrs Moshie.' On cue, Mrs Moshie grunted in her sleep. 'You know, in case she wakes up.'

'You sure?' Mum switched Stevie to the other hip as he tried to wiggle down. 'You're gonna hate this movie. It's all singing and dancing and terrible music.'

'Oh, yeah, I know,' I said. 'But whatever.'

'Suit yourself. But don't leave this rug, and wake Mrs Moshie if you need anything.'

'Sure, Mum. See ya.'

She kissed me on the head and said something else, but I didn't hear it because I was right there on the streets of Baltimore with Tracy Turnblad, riding that rubbish truck.

I didn't move for the next two hours. I'm not sure I even blinked. It was my very first musical. It was the most amazing thing I'd ever seen. And it flipped my entire taste in music upside down.

'You look like your head's about to explode, Mac!'

I snap out of my trip down memory lane and look up to see Casey Wu standing in front of me.

'Hey,' I say, then spin around to look at the plaque on the bench behind me. 'Oh, this is your mum's bench. Sorry, I'll go.'

'What? No,' says Casey, pushing me back down. 'I don't own this seat, Mac, it's for everybody. It's a great place for thinking, and it looks like you've got a lot of thinking to do. I'm actually on my way to rehearsals. Bit tardy today, sorry.'

'Bit what?'

'Late. I'm running late. New favourite word.'

'Ah!' I nod. 'Got it. Oh, rehearsal's been moved to a warehouse down the street.'

Casey nods. 'Yeah, Zeke messaged Dad about the theatre. Total bummer, huh?'

'Yeah, and it's gonna be closed for ages so we can't do the musical there at all. We might have to cancel.'

'No way!' Casey says, taking a seat beside me. 'We can figure something out.' She runs through all the options I've already come up with and tossed aside. 'We have to be missing something.' Casey pulls out her notebook. 'Watterson is a small town, but it's not THAT small. There have to be plenty of places we could do a show. What do we need?'

'A lot of space.'

Casey writes it down.

'Lights.'

She writes that too.

'Somewhere we can build sets and leave them. Preferably somewhere there's been a show or event before so we're not starting from scratch. Somewhere that can fit the whole town over a week. Somewhere central for everyone to get to. And most importantly, somewhere we can actually get permission to use.'

Casey looks at her list and chews on her pen. She leans back on the bench and looks up through the leaves of the tree hanging over our heads. I join her and we sit in silence, willing Casey's thinking bench to work its magic.

'We need Kathy,' says Casey. 'She's the town problem solver.'

'Well, right now she's in rehearsals, becoming the town's musical tour guide.'

Casey smiles. 'Shame her Lego house isn't a bit bigger, she'd let us use that.'

I nod. 'Shame we haven't got a bit more Lego, we could just build a new theatre here in Brennan Park.'

Casey springs up like she's been zapped. 'Mac, that's it!'

'What's it? I was joking. Do you know how much Lego it would take to build a theatre?'

'But who says a theatre needs a roof?'

'Huh?'

Casey throws her arms out wide, spinning around. 'This is your theatre. Brennan Park! We've had town fairs and stuff here, so we know it can accommodate lights and a stage and food and drinks. You could build the different sets throughout the park.' Standing in the middle of the grass, Casey points around wildly. 'The Funky Anchovy could go over there, Balthazar Theatre over there, the town hall is already here and the set for Brennan Park is a no-brainer.'

I leap up off the seat too. I can totally see it. 'We wouldn't even have to build Kathy's house – we could use the real thing. And Kathy could lead the audience around the park from scene to scene, like a travelling show.'

'Yes!' Casey's eyes are wide with excitement now. 'Mac, it would be brilliant. An open air show. We could map out a mini version of the town.'

'I love it!' I say. 'It would be like Shakespeare in the park.'

She stops. 'Like what?'

'Never mind,' I say, laughing. 'Open air theatre. Yes!' I stop. 'But wait, how are we ever going to get permission for that?'

Casey looks at me like my brain has fallen out. 'Mac, my dad is the mayor! If anyone can sweet-talk this plan into action, it's me!'

'You would do that?'

'Are you kidding me? You think you're the only one who loves Ms Fox? Or Mr Dinesh? Or even Mr Hubbard, for that matter? None of us want to see them go, Mac.'

'Everyone knows about that?'

'Nothing stays a secret in Watterson,' Casey says, giving me a playful shove. 'Surely you know that by now? That's why everyone is so on board. You're not doing this alone.'

I grin at her. I've always been a bit of a loner, but I'm starting to realise that's one of the cool things about this town – there's always someone around when you need them.

'Thanks, Casey. It would be awesome if you could talk to your dad.'

'Consider it done! And Mac?'

'Yeah?'

'A lot of people are with you on this. Reach out a bit. You'll be surprised how many people reach back.'

I nod. 'Thanks, Casey. I will.'

She gives me a quick hug. 'Gotta run. I'll talk to Dad tonight and let you know.'

I watch as she runs off towards the warehouse and I give the park bench a little pat.

'Thanks, thinking bench. Solid work!'

A small twig falls from the tree above, hitting me on the head.

'Ow!' I rub my head and get up. 'Okay, message received. Back to rehearsal.'

When I get back to the warehouse, the vibe has changed.

'What's going on?' I ask Flynn. 'Why is everyone just sitting around?'

'Word about the gherkin theatre has spread. Whoop. Now that we've got nowhere wheeee to do the show, it's kinda stop got everyone a bit gherkin deflated.'

'Well, they better get reinflated!' I say, striding across the warehouse and snatching the megaphone from Mr Deery.

'Hey!' Mr Deery blinks at his now empty hand. 'What are you –'

'I'll bring it back, Mr D!' I yell over my shoulder.

'Okay, but you could've asked nicely,' he mumbles.

I've got to get everyone back to work but there's something I have to do first. I find Ms Fox leafing through the music sheets.

'Ms Fox?'

She looks up at me. 'Yeah, Mac.'

'I know about your job: I was in the cupboard. I wasn't spying, I promise, just cleaning up.'

She smiles at me. 'I know. Mr Deery told me.'

'He did?'

'Sure. There's a teacher code. Plus he totally can't keep a secret. Worst liar ever!' She takes my hand.

'I know what you're doing here, with the musical. And I think you're incredible.'

It's hard to look at her. She's so kind even when she's about to get booted out of the school. 'I'm really sorry about your job. And angry. You're the best teacher ever.'

She squeezes my hand. 'Thanks, Mac. I'm just sad the kids won't be learning music any more. Or drama. Or art.'

I roll my eyes. 'Just a masterclass in creative action. What even is that?'

Ms Fox scoffs. 'Nobody knows. But look at this.' She waves her hand at everyone in front of us. '*This* is the arts. It brings people together, brings them joy. How do people not see that?'

'I see it.'

Ms Fox smiles sadly. 'That's why we need more people like you, Mac.'

I grip the megaphone. 'Don't worry. I'm gonna save the arts and your job, Ms Fox. Just watch me!' I give her rock hands and march to the centre of the warehouse.

Sitting to the side is the prop treasure chest made for the backyard scene where Tess and Toby find the million dollars. I pull it out and climb on top. Raising the megaphone to my mouth, I get everybody's attention.

'Everyone off your butts and gather around!'

I wait while everyone slowly drags themselves over to where I am. I've got to get some fire into these peeps!

'So you've all heard about the theatre. Yes, it sucks that our venue is gone, but in the end a theatre is just a place. It's what we're creating here –' I wave my hand around the shelves of cat food and dog chews. 'What we're creating together – that matters. WHY we're doing it matters. The arts matter, and our teachers matter, and that hasn't changed.'

I look around me. 'We're gonna fix the venue problem, I promise – don't worry about that. What I need right now is for you to get off your butts and get back to rehearsing so we can make this the best musical this town has ever seen.'

Tess Heckleston raises her hand. 'Isn't it kinda the first musical this town has ever seen? So by default we've already achieved that?'

Toby glares at her and she slowly lowers her hands. 'Not an important thing to point out right now? Got it.'

'We need to get back to work so we can save the arts!'

Casey Wu grins at me and gives me a thumbs-up. 'Save the arts!' she yells.

Zeke and Cookie join in. 'Save the arts! Save the arts!' Soon the entire cast and crew are chanting and the words echo around the warehouse.

I catch Flynn's eye. He looks pretty proud. I feel proud.

'Now GET TO IT!'

A huge cheer fills the space and the crowd splits up, everyone going back to their jobs.

Casey grins at me and points to the megaphone. 'How good is that thing?'

I hop down off the treasure chest. 'The power! I love it.'

'Right?'

Mr Deery pats me on the back and peels the megaphone out of my grip. 'All right there, boss. I'll just take that back now if that's okay?'

I let him take it, a little sad to see it go.

'Nice speech, Mac!' he says, then speaks into the megaphone. 'Let's run through "There's No Place Like Watterson", everybody.'

I pick up my guitar and join the band, ready to rock out!

ACT THREE

Scene One

The Streets of Watterson

The entire town pulls together in preparation for *Watterson: The Musical*. Every person plays a role, determined to stop the Arts Fiasco. The underestimated townsfolk reveal an array of hidden talents as favours are called in and people step up.

'In Watterson'

(to the tune of 'On Broadway' from *Beautiful: The Carole King Musical*)

They say the car headlights are bright in
Watterson (in Watterson).
They say there's always parking fines to pay
But when you've got a show to do
And the theatre is drowned in poo
You don't just give it up and walk away
(in Watterson).

They say the streets are old and cracked
in Watterson (in Watterson).
They say the people in the town are too
But that is not quite fair at all
'Cos when you need them, you just call
And they'll be there to help and see you
through.

The next few weeks are a tornado of showtunes. Mayor Wu thinks it'll be fine to use Brennan Park for our 'wandering' musical. He needs to file some applications and permits and other stuff I know nothing about, but for now we're charging ahead.

I'm more than a bit worried we won't make enough money to stop the Arts Fiasco though. It has occurred to me that Watterson isn't a very big place, and I feel like half the town is either **IN** the musical or working on it. Does that leave many people to fill the audience? Will we even make much money?

So far, everything we need has been donated. Whether it's time, equipment or skills, people are offering what they can. It's pretty amazing, to be honest. Flynn's dad even knows a woman who donated all the lights for us to use for the run of the show and Giuseppe's son got a guy he knows to provide generators for free.

And Mr Deery? Mr D is something else. Sometimes I think maybe he's wasted at Watterson Primary. He's even dragged Jennifer Heckleston into the team. She's had to shut down Balthazar Theatre. Apparently it's gonna cost heaps to repair the theatre and 'get it up to code', which means fixing enough that they can reopen and let people back in again. Chances are it will just get demolished and sold. Jennifer's devastated, so Mr Deery has roped her in to help with the show to get her mind off things.

There are really only two people in all of Watterson that I haven't seen helping in one way or another: Mrs Keiren and . . . Mum.

Mrs Keiren is no surprise. She clearly doesn't care about the arts, or us kids or probably anything except whether we wash our hands before we touch the library books. I bet she's locked away in her office counting coins and deciding which poor teacher's job she's going to axe next. How she can spend so much time making sure our socks are pulled up and so little time saving the jobs of awesome teachers like Ms Fox is something I'll never understand.

But Mum? Well, that's my fault. She probably *would* be here helping if she knew about the musical, but I still haven't had the guts to tell her. I've been waiting for someone else to do it, but this whole thing has sort of made me realise Mum doesn't actually have many friends. She's pretty much at work or hanging out with me and Stevie. And lately she's been so stressed out trying to figure out a way to save the live music at The Garage. I don't want to add to her load.

Well, that and I'm still not ready to admit to liking Broadway. You might think I'm being ridiculous about it, but the other day she read an article in the local newspaper about Balthazar Theatre closing and said . . .

'Of course, they're all worried about the theatre snobs not having somewhere to go in their mink coats, but I don't see anyone writing an article about the town losing its ONLY live music venue. At least at The Garage you could hear some *real* music!'

Mum then tossed the newspaper across the kitchen and turned up Fleetwood Mac really loud. I dragged Stevie into my room and we played Snap, leaving Mum to belt out a few songs at the top of her lungs. It's how she deals with stuff.

I will tell her soon though, I swear. Just not right now.

'I don't know why we're here,' repeats Mr Deery.

Flynn, Kathy, Binita, Giuseppe and I stand in a circle around Mr Deery, glaring at him. We've all rushed to Town Hall at the request of his urgent text, only to discover he doesn't know why we're here either. 'Mr Wu just said to meet him.'

'Maybe there's a problem with the show?' suggests Giuseppe.

'We don't know that,' says Kathy. Mr Piddles hides in her coat pocket. Maybe he's thinking the same thing as me – are ferrets allowed in official council buildings?

Binita sighs. 'Well, you don't generally have "urgent meetings" to announce everything is going smoothly.'

This panics me a little. Binita would know, after all. She looks like an 'urgent meeting' kind of person.

'Do we actually have gherkin confirmed permission to put the stop show on in whoop Brennan Park?'

We all look at Mr Deery. He turns a little white. 'Henry assured me it wouldn't be a problem.'

'A problem with the slime machine!' shouts Flynn. 'Sorry gherkin, I'm nervous. The show's in the toilet, press flush.'

'That's it, isn't it?' I say. 'The show – it's cancelled. After all this work.' I'm kind of glad I didn't tell Mum about it now.

Mr Deery waves his hands. 'Let's not get ahead of ourselves before we hear what the mayor has to say.' But I can tell he's worried.

It's less than two weeks until the musical premieres. Posters are going up all over town, dress rehearsals are in full swing and, to be honest, I'm really proud and excited about the show.

A guy called Claudio comes out into the foyer and calls us into Mayor Wu's office. Mr Wu gestures for us to all sit down on the couches in a little parlour area set up to one side of the room. Much less formal than his big wooden desk.

'Please take a seat, everyone,' he says.

'Don't sit on the cactus!' I can tell Flynn is nervous. 'Sorry,' he says. 'I have gherkin Tourette's wheeee!'

Mr Wu nods. 'No cactuses here, I promise.' He smiles warmly and waits for us all to sit before joining us.

'Thanks for coming. My daughter, Casey, has been keeping me up to date on the progress of your show. It sounds amazing; she's been rehearsing her song non-stop.'

'Thanks, Mayor Wu,' says Mr Deery. 'Casey and the Green Peas have been a huge help in organising volunteers and getting businesses to help out.

And she organised an Auslan interpreter for the show –'

'And she spoke to you,' I interrupt. 'Without the park, we wouldn't have anywhere to actually put the show on.'

I watch Mr Wu's face fall and I know what's coming.

'Yes, about that . . .'

I knew it. It's all over. I try to prepare myself for the bad news.

'The universe has been cancelled. Tell the pigeons.'

Kathy passes Mr Piddles to Flynn. The ferret curls up in Flynn's lap and accepts the frantic pats Flynn gives him. 'Sorry again whoop. Bit gherkin nervous. Never been in a stop mayor's gherkin office before wheeee.'

Mr Wu gives Mr Piddles a pat too. Apparently, ferrets *are* allowed indoors after all. 'Don't be nervous,' says Mr Wu. 'It's not like the principal's office.' He winks at Flynn.

'Now, there is a bit of a hiccup with the permit . . .'

'I knew it,' says Binita. 'We can't use the park. The show's cancelled.' She pulls her phone out and starts tapping. I'm wondering if she's cancelling all those favours she called in.

'No, not exactly,' says Mayor Wu. Binita stops tapping and looks up.

'What do you mean, "not exactly"?' asks Kathy.

'Sounds like mayor talk for "exactly that but I'm going to talk my way around it",' says Giuseppe, folding his arms across his chest and glaring at the mayor.

Mr Wu raises his hands. 'Look, I know your previous mayor experience was, how can I say, less than desirable –'

'You mean she was a swindling dirtbag who didn't give a rat's tail about us!' Giuseppe tilts his head, daring Mayor Wu to argue.

'Pin the rat's tail on the hippo!' Flynn hugs Mr Piddles a little closer. 'Sorry.'

'That may be another way to put it,' says Mr Wu. 'But that's not the case now. I have looked into the permit options for your show and it can go ahead in two weeks, but with a few conditions.'

I let out a big sigh and realise I've been holding my breath this whole time. The show's not cancelled. Surely we can work with conditions.

But Binita's eyes narrow. 'What conditions?'

Mr Wu swallows and looks at us apologetically. 'There can only be one show.'

'What?' I say.

'And you can't charge for tickets.'

Our mouths all drop at once. Mr Deery manages to get his working again first. 'But, Henry, that doesn't make sense. Why?'

'Look, it's a lot of bureaucracy, but essentially I can get the permit pushed through if it's a one-off charitable event rather than a for-profit extended run.'

'But aren't you the mayor?' I say. 'Casey said you can make anything happen.'

Mr Wu leans back. 'While I am flattered by my daughter's infinite faith in my influence, that is not quite how it works. I can't just have the final say in everything – we've seen the trouble that can get us into. I know this is a compromise, but it does mean the show can still go ahead.'

I can't hold it in any longer. 'But we'll never get the money to save Ms Fox with one show and no ticket sales, let alone Mr Dinesh and Mr Hubbard. What's the point of all this hard work if it's just going to be a failure anyway?'

Mr Wu stares at me, confused by my outburst. 'What do you mean, "save Ms Fox"?'

I look at Mr Deery. The decision to cut the arts program from Watterson Primary is pretty common knowledge on the Watterson grapevine by now, but it still hasn't officially been announced.

Mr Deery nods. 'Go ahead, Mac.'

And I spill.

I tell the mayor about how the whole reason we're doing the musical is to stop the Arts Fiasco. About the cuts to the school funding and the end of the arts subjects and the teachers' jobs. And once I'm on a roll, it's hard to stop. I tell him about Balthazar Theatre being destroyed and the live music venue at The Garage being turned into a pokies room and how nobody seems to care that the arts are disappearing from Watterson.

'I hear adults talking all the time about how kids are glued to their screens and don't appreciate art and music and theatre anymore but **YOU** are the ones taking it away from us!' I point my finger at the mayor and then realise how rude it is and quickly pull it back. 'Well, not **YOU**, you, but you know, the greater you.'

'You get in the boot on lizard day!' We look at Flynn, who is now pointing at the mayor too. 'Sorry, but he's gherkin right whoop.'

'Wait a minute,' says Mayor Wu. 'I think we need to back this up a bit. There's clearly a lot more going on here than just a musical performance, am I right?'

I nod. 'A lot more.'

We spend the rest of the afternoon in the mayor's office. He cancels his meetings and listens to us. To me. And I tell him all the ways his town is going down the cultural toilet.

By the time I get home that afternoon, I'm exhausted. It's a good kind of exhausted, though.

I feel heard. Almost lighter after unloading all the things that seem so unfair, especially to someone who can maybe do something about them.

We've agreed to a one-night-only show and, even though we can't charge for tickets, we *are* allowed to collect donations, so we can still raise money for Ms Fox. Mayor Wu said he'd look into what was going on with the school funding, and the theatre and even The Garage.

So, as I push my front door open, I'm feeling pretty good. Until . . .

Mum and Ms Fox are standing in our kitchen, staring at me.

I freeze. This is weird. Like really weird.

'What?' I ask cautiously, not sure I really want to know.

Mum grabs something off the kitchen bench and holds it up in front of me. I read the words *'Watterson: The Musical'* in big gold letters across the top.

Oh. I guess with everything going on, I kinda forgot the posters were going up today. And more importantly, I forgot what was written on the bottom of them.

LYRICS BY MAC COOPER
MUSIC BY FLYNN VANDERBERG

'Oh . . . that,' I say, hanging my head.

'How could you not tell me about this, Mac?' Mum asks.

I can't look at her. She's either going to be angry or disappointed and I can't really do either right now. Today has been a lot.

'I'm sorry, Mac,' says Ms Fox. 'I had no idea you hadn't told her. I thought I'd bring your mum her own copy, hot off the press.'

I don't blame Ms Fox even the tiniest bit. This was always coming, and I knew it.

'I was gonna tell you, Mum, I promise. I was just waiting for the right time.'

'And when was that going to be?' she says, her voice raising. 'Opening night?'

I shrug. 'Maybe.' I try to gauge Mum's anger levels. Mad Mum is usually pretty easy to read. But she looks more hurt than anything. And that kills me.

'And Ms Fox says this is the new music group? This is where you've been with Flynn? Writing and rehearsing a . . .' She looks at the poster again, trying to assess it like it's a unicorn or something. ' . . . a musical?'

'This is why I didn't tell you! I've been writing a musical, not out robbing little old ladies. You don't have to look so disappointed.'

Her eyes soften. 'I'm not disappointed, Mac. I'm confused. I thought you wanted to be a rock star.'

I take a deep breath. This is it. I've rehearsed these words so many times. I brace myself to say them out loud.

'*You* wanted me to be a rock star. I just wanted to make you happy.'

Mum shakes her head, looking at everything except me. 'But if you focused on your guitar you could join a band, or even better, start your own, and have an actual career in real music.'

'Like you wanted?' I ask softly.

She barely takes a breath. 'I could have really been somebody if my parents had given me half the support and encouragement I give you! My parents wouldn't let me take singing lessons, even when I got a job and paid for them myself!'

'I know, Mum,' I say. 'You told me. "If it's not classical, then it's just not music" – Grandma's favourite saying. But it wasn't Grandma's place to tell you how to rock . . . right?'

'Right rock! Rock the right way.' We all turn to face Stevie, standing in the doorway. 'There's no right way to rock!' Stevie gives us rock hands and wanders off to the lounge room singing 'Dance Monkey'.

I turn to Mum. She looks shocked. And a bit sad. 'Oh no,' she says softly. 'I'm just like them, aren't I?' She buries her face in her hands. 'I'm so sorry, Mac. I . . . it's just . . . you're SO good at guitar.' She looks to Ms Fox for support. 'Isn't he?'

Ms Fox shifts uncomfortably on the spot. 'Well, yes, but – '

'If you think I'm good at guitar, you should see me write musicals, Mum. I'm awesome at it.'

Saying it out loud – saying it to *her* – makes me feel like I've just thrown the red velvet curtain wide open, bared my soul to her and now I'm standing there, centre stage, right under the spotlight . . . hoping for applause.

'You are?' Mum asks quietly.

I smile and nod. 'Actually, I totally rock at it, don't I, Ms Fox?'

She smiles gently. 'You sure do, kiddo.'

Mum reaches out for me. 'Of course you do. You rock at everything, Mac.'

I move into Mum's arms and soak up her hug. She squeezes me extra hard.

Ms Fox shifts on her feet. 'Look, I might go,' she mumbles. 'Bye, Nikki. See ya, Mac.' She walks over to me. Handing me a USB, she whispers, 'Flynn asked me to give you this. It's the one we talked about. Might come in handy.' I grin and slip it into the back of my jeans.

We stay quiet as Ms Fox leaves.

'Does it make you happy?' Mum asks.

'Musical theatre?'

She nods.

I smile. 'So happy. Like nothing I've ever done before. Like there's something in my chest that gets so big that it feels like it might not fit anymore. You know what I mean?'

Mum nods. 'I know exactly what you mean.' Taking my hands, she looks me straight in the eyes. 'I owe you an apology, Mac. I want a lot of things for you in this world and I got a bit caught up in that. But most of all, more than anything, I want you to be happy.'

'I know, Mum.'

She shakes her head. 'No, I don't think you do. I don't want you to make *me* happy. There's a difference. It's your life, not mine. Live it your way. And I will always be your biggest fan.'

I throw my arms around her again. 'Even if it takes me to Broadway?'

'Wherever it takes you. Stevie and I will always be front row.'

'Front row! Row the boat!' Stevie yells from the lounge room.

Mum leads me to the kitchen table and we both sit down. 'Right, I'm listening. Really, this time. Tell me everything.'

And I do. I tell her everything.

When I finish, Mum's mouth is hanging slightly open. 'So you and Flynn wrote an *entire* musical?'

'Yup.'

'And got the entire town on board?'

'Pretty much.'

She pauses. 'So, is it, like, tap shoes and tights and stuff?'

I burst out laughing. 'Mum! Do you not even know what a musical is?'

She shrugs. 'I guess not. I don't think I've ever seen one.'

I grin at her. 'Well, we're gonna fix that right now.' I drag Mum into the lounge room and plonk her down on the couch. Stevie doesn't complain when I plug Flynn's USB into the TV and click on the file.

'What's this?' Mum asks.

'Your first ever musical. Flynn's mum had a video of an old dress rehearsal. But don't worry, I think it's one you're going to like.'

'What's it called?'

'*School of Rock*,' I say, joining Mum on the couch. Stevie crawls up quietly on the other side and lays his head in her lap. 'Rock school,' he mumbles softly as she strokes his cheek.

Mum puts her arm around me and I snuggle into her. As she twists my hair around her finger like she used to do when I was little, the band No Vacancy introduces her to the wonderful world of musical theatre.

ACT THREE
Scene Two

Watterson Town Hall

The people of Watterson make their way to Brennan Park. A crowd forms around Town Hall, full of people there to show their support on the opening night of *Watterson: The Musical*. As the crowd marches forward, each person drops a coin or note into the donation box.

'Do You Hear Our People Sing?'

(to the tune of 'Do You Hear the People Sing?' from *Les Misérables*)

Do you hear our people sing?
Singing the song that's in their hearts.
It is the voices of the people
Who demand to have their arts.

When the culture of your town
Echoes a tumbleweed of loss
Then you'll see, we won't back down
At whatever cost!

The town hall is buzzing with activity. The big night came around so fast that I can barely remember the blur of the last two weeks. But it's here, it's real and it's chaos! People are running everywhere and you can feel the energy in the air. Mum zooms past me pushing a trolley of water. She looks around, wide-eyed, and mouths 'AMAZING!' to me before dashing off. She took the whole weekend off work to help out with the show. Mrs Moshie is looking after Stevie and will bring him to the performance later tonight.

Mum has done a total backflip with her attitude towards musicals. Well, at least with her attitude towards MY musical. This whole time I thought she hated anything that wasn't rock. But it turns out she can get on board with anything I love. Once I'd finally told her how much it meant to me, she wanted to know, and hear, everything. She's been playing the entire musical around the house non-stop. I'm pretty sure she knows every word to every song by now. I even had to ask the other day if we could take a break from it and listen to some Fleetwood Mac.

'Mac!' Casey Wu's hand lands on my shoulder. 'Mr Deery suggested maybe we should take the audience *behind* the Lego house after the ferret song instead of leading them down the path. He thinks the crowd transition will work better.'

I flick through the script to the map of audience movements stapled at the back. 'But then they'll be on the wrong side of the grey ironbark for "Bench Your Thoughts". Keep it like it is but ask Kathy to start the song on her guitar to get the crowd moving. Then the band can join in when she reaches her final position. Kathy can handle the transition.'

Casey nods. 'I'll let Mr D know.'

I'm not too worried about leading the audience around the park. To be fair, there won't be that many people – almost half of Watterson is IN the show by now, so we're not expecting a huge audience.

'Whatcha thinking, kiddo?' Ms Fox appears beside me.

I grin at her and shrug. 'Dunno. It's just all . . . really cool.'

'Sure is. You're really something, Mac.'

'Nah, not me. Everyone. I just had a little idea, but this – this is everyone.'

'Of course. But someone has to start a great idea. Like planting a seed. I think Watterson really needed this, Mac. I know I did.'

I look up at her. The town might have needed a musical, but with a small audience and only being able to take donations, the show won't be able to do what I hoped it would. 'I don't think we're gonna make enough money to save your job, Ms Fox. I'm so sorry.'

She scruffs my hair. 'Don't you dare, Mac Cooper. This show, working on it, watching the town come together, this is the *best* farewell I could've asked for.'

I'd always thought of our musical as a way to make money, and in that sense it looks like it's going to be an epic fail. But Ms Fox looks genuinely happy. All three soon-to-be-out-of-a-job teachers do. Now *that* I hadn't expected. Mr Hubbard has joined forces with Mr D and they have directed this production into a masterpiece and Mr Dinesh has had so much fun working on the sets that he hops from foot to foot like a little kid every time he gets to rehearsal.

Ms Fox gives my shoulder a squeeze. 'I'll never forget what you did, Mac.'

'And I'll never forget you.'

Ms Fox gives me a little shove. 'You'd better not!'

'OMG gherkin!' Flynn is bolting towards us, waving his phone in the air. 'Mac! MAC! Twitter has a Facebook account!'

Mr Deery comes from the other direction. 'Mac! How did you do it?'

'What?' I have zero idea what they're on about.

'You've gone gherkin viral!' Flynn shoves his phone in my face, so close that my eyes can't focus and I feel like the screen is blinding me. I grab his hand and push it back. My eyes adjust and I recognise the little musical note from TikTok.

'What? I don't –'

'Gherkin watch it. Whoop.' Flynn shoves the phone forward again.

'Stop it!' I say, pushing the phone away. 'I can't watch it when it's halfway up my nose.'

Frustrated, Flynn turns the phone towards himself. 'TikTok is planning a zombie invasion. No gherkin. Wrap your dad in a lamington. Argh. This is not a wasabi sandwich. Mac! Velociraptor pie. Whoop!' The phone is back in my face.

I take it from him and read. I can feel my eyeballs grow until they're almost too big for their sockets.

'What is it?' asks Ms Fox.

I look at Flynn, who's bouncing and ticcing with excitement. 'Someone took a video of our rehearsal, and it's gone viral,' I say slowly.

'Yes! Gherkin!' Flynn points at me and at the roof at the same time. 'That's what I was gherkin trying to stop say. Boogers!'

I press play on the video. My throat dries up when I see myself, standing in the Pet Food warehouse on the treasure chest with a megaphone to my mouth. My voice plays out of the phone speaker. 'What I need right now is for you to get off your butts and start rehearsing so we can make this the best musical this town has ever seen.' This is followed by everyone chanting 'SAVE THE ARTS!' and then cuts to our rehearsal of 'There's No Place Like Watterson'.

'But who? . . . How?' I ask.

'No gherkin idea!' says Flynn. 'But it's everywhere – TikTok, You-gherkin-Tube, Twitter and wheeee everywhere else.'

Ms Fox takes the phone. 'Ten thousand views?! What?'

'How is that even possible?' I ask.

Ms Fox clicks through to Twitter and starts scanning tweets. 'Looks like it's been shared by just about every actor and musician in Australia, Mac!' She scrolls down.

I take the phone back and read the tweet above my video. 'Flynn! This tweet is from Kay Angelos!'

'Throw a sock in the deep fryer!'

I try to focus on the text. 'Listen to this – "If you're in the area with nothing to do on Saturday night, can I suggest swinging by Watterson to check out the premiere of *Watterson: The Musical*? Entirely written and composed by two kids, Flynn Vanderberg and Mac Cooper, it promises to be a one-night wonder so don't miss it!"'

Flynn gives me a peace sign followed by a thumbs-up. 'And she has almost fifteen thousand followers.'

It's Mr Deery's turn to snatch the phone. 'Well, that explains it, I guess.'

'Explains what?' I ask.

He waves us over and we follow him to the entrance to Town Hall, where a bunch of the cast and crew are already crowded together, peeking through the doors.

'Sorry, everyone, can we squeeze through?' Mr Deery pushes towards the doors and Flynn and I look outside.

'What the? Gherkin.'

'Whoa!' Outside, hundreds of people are gathering – like hundreds and hundreds – in a huge line that runs down the side of the park. I watch as people pass the box labelled 'Gold Coin

Donation' around, trying to squeeze notes inside when it's already busting full.

Mr Deery looks around. 'Tess! Tess Heckleston!' Tess comes running over with Toby in tow.

'Yeah, Mr Deery?'

'Can you please switch out the donation box? Maybe see if you can find something a little larger. Looks like we might have a bigger crowd than we thought.'

'Sure thing, Mr D!' Tess goes to run off when Mr Deery stops her.

'Maybe take Toby with you. And make sure the money gets to Ms Mezher.' His eyes narrow. 'All of it!'

Tess rolls her eyes. 'It was one time, Mr D. ONE TIME! Haven't you heard of forgive and forget?'

Mr Deery nods. 'Of course, Tess. I'm sorry. Off you go.' As soon as she heads off, Mr Deery waves at Toby and mouths, 'Go with her!'

Toby salutes and they disappear.

Mr Deery ushers everyone away from the door, then closes it, leaning his back against it. 'Okay, everyone, looks like the crowd will be a little bigger than we thought, but we still have the same jobs to do. I'll let the ushers know and we'll see if we can get some extra hands on deck. Everyone back to your places.'

The crowd moves off, leaving just me, Flynn, Mr D and Ms Fox in the foyer.

'Kay Angelos tweeted my whoop name. *My* gherkin name.' Flynn shakes his head in disbelief. 'I think my gherkin life just stop peaked.'

'But who made that video in the first place?' I ask. 'It's not like Kay Angelos was at our rehearsal.'

Mr Deery shrugs. 'I have no idea, but it was just the publicity we needed.'

'How are we going to manage that many people?' says Ms Fox. 'We only have a handful of ushers out there and most of them are kids. Our plan was for an audience of maybe a couple of hundred at best. It looks like over a thousand people out there!'

Mr Deery *does* look worried, which makes me worried.

The door behind us shakes as someone tries to push it from outside. He turns around and opens it a crack. Tess Heckleston stands on the steps.

'Where's the money, Tess?'

She rolls her eyes again. I think her eyes spend more time at the top of her head than anywhere else.

'Mr D, you really have to let it go. I haven't put one foot wrong . . . again . . . all year. Ms Mezher has it. Plus I think you've got bigger problems to worry about – like crowd control?'

'Yes, we were just discussing that.'

'Well, I'd like to introduce you to a . . . can I say "friend of mine"?' Tess asks someone over her shoulder. 'Are we friends now?'

A police officer steps forward. 'I think "friends" is a reasonable description of us these days,' he says.

'Awesome! So, Mr Deery, this is Senior Detective McKenzie. Detective Mac, this is Mr D!'

Detective McKenzie glares at Tess and she cowers a little. 'Oh, not nickname kind of friends yet? Got it. Sorry.'

Detective McKenzie shakes hands with Mr Deery. 'We heard you have a few more people than expected and thought maybe we could help? The station and I came to see the show, of course, but we do have quite a bit of useful experience as . . . ushers, of a sort.'

A look of relief washes over Mr Deery's face. 'That would be amazing, Detective McKenzie. Yes. Please. We need all the help we can get.'

The police officer nods. 'We've got it covered. Have a good show.'

He walks off to join his officers and starts giving instructions. Tess squeezes inside.

'Good work, Tess,' says Mr Deery.

'Doing what I can to wear down that trouble-maker reputation.'

Mr Deery claps his hands. 'All right, another problem solved. On with the show!'

'Ah, not quite!' Mr Hubbard runs up to join us. 'We have a much bigger problem at hand. Disastrous, in fact.'

'What could be wrong now?' I ask.

Mr Hubbard turns a little white. 'It's fifteen minutes to showtime and no one can find Kathy.'

I instantly regret asking. 'But she OPENS the show!'

'She gherkin CARRIES the show whoop!' adds Flynn.

Mr Hubbard swallows loudly. 'Not if we can't find her, she doesn't.'

You have *got* to be kidding me! How can we lose the star of the show fifteen minutes before we go on? Casey walks past with her megaphone and I snatch it out of her hands.

'Attention, everybody. Anyone who isn't doing something one hundred per cent vital to the show starting on time, you have a new task. **FIND KATHY!**'

Apparently, I don't have to explain the concept of Kathy being lost because everyone spreads like ants and begins hunting.

I turn to my teachers. 'Well, you lot too. Off you go. No Kathy, no show. Let's go!'

The teachers spring into action and I grab Flynn's arm. 'You're with me.'

'Marsupials are overrated!' Flynn yells as I drag him off.

'Any luck?' I ask.

It's literally five minutes until showtime and Kathy has vanished off the face of the planet.

Everyone shakes their heads. I grab my hair. 'What are we going to do?'

Then I hear it.

In a very big universe, there's a fairly
big planet
With a country that's all girt by sea.
To the East there's a state, and
somewhere in the middle
Is a town where you might meet me!

I spin around to see Mum dragging a pallet backstage. She's singing to herself. Singing *our* musical. Just like she has been non-stop for the past two weeks.

'Mum!'

She stops and spins around. 'Mac, honey! You ready? You must be so excited!'

'Excited? Try panicked. Where have you been?'

Mum points out the back. 'In the loading dock. Is everything okay?'

I run over and grab her hand. 'No, everything is NOT okay. Kathy's missing.'

Mum's mouth drops open. She knows the show so well now that I don't have explain that no Kathy means no show.

'Oh no, Mac. That's terrible. Can I help?'

I nod.

'Want me to go look for her?'

I shake my head.

'What then?'

'I need you to go on, Mum.'

'On?'

'Yes. On stage. To replace Kathy.'

'ME?' She drops the palette handle to the floor. 'I can't be in a musical!'

'Why not?' I say. 'You're an awesome singer. You know all the words. And well, you'd be brilliant!'

She hesitates. 'You think so?'

'I know so. And top of that, this might be the biggest crowd you've ever sung in front of. Do you want to miss that opportunity?'

Mum scoffs. 'Mac, you know I sung in front of almost three hundred people at the Pambala Music Festival back when I was in the band.'

'Oh yeah?' I grab Mum's hand and drag her over to the doors, cracking them so she can see outside.

'Holy cow!' Mum's eyes bulge as she looks out over the crowd gathering in Brennan Park.

I smile. 'Last count puts it well over two thousand, and they're still coming.'

'And they all came to see a musical?' She turns to me. '*Your* musical?'

'Apparently so. But there won't be a musical unless I put someone onstage in five minutes to sing the opening number.'

Mum takes one more look out the door. 'I'll do it.'

Wrapping my arms around her, I give her a big hug. 'Thanks, Mum.'

She squeezes me back. 'You know I'd do anything for you, right?'

'I do.'

'Then let's rock! But please do find Kathy because I know the first song really well and after that . . . let's just say, not so confident.'

'You bet,' I say. 'Casey!'

Casey appears by my side in that magic Casey Wu way. 'Yes, boss?'

'Mum's gonna do Kathy's opening number. Can you –'

'Get her to wardrobe? Made up? Mic-ed up and to side stage? On it.'

They disappear together and I turn back to face the cast and crew gathered around me.

'Well, what are you all staring at? We have a show to put on.'

Flynn moves to stand next to me. 'Yeah we gherkin do. Places, everybody! It's time for a tap dancing lizard!' Flynn shakes his head. 'No it's gherkin not. Although that could whoop make the next show. IT'S GHERKIN SHOWTIME!'

ACT THREE

Scene Three

Brennan Park

NIKKI COOPER stands in Brennan Park, illuminated by a spotlight. A crowd of thousands watches on in awe as she sings the opening number to *Watterson: The Musical*. Her voice echoes through the night, mesmerising even the possums.

'The Watto Spirit' from

Watterson: The Musical

And so the residents of this quaint and
quiet little town
Are neither very quaint nor very quiet.
If you try to double-cross them or mess
with their home
You very well may start a riot.

And so tonight I welcome each and every
one of you
To take a little tour of my town.
Because if there's one thing you should
know about dear Watterson . . .
You can't keep the Watto spirit down.

Watching Mum, I'm almost in tears. She is SO good. You wouldn't have guessed for one second that her only rehearsals had been in our kitchen. She struts across the park in Kathy's big coat, a stuffed Mr Piddles attached to the shoulder, drawing the audience in as she hits every note perfectly. I couldn't be more proud.

'She's great, isn't she?'

I spin around to see Kathy standing casually behind me.

'Kathy! Where have you been? We've been looking everywhere for you.'

'Yes, well, Mr Piddles and I had some important things to attend to.'

'More important than the opening number of our show on its opening night?'

'I knew you'd find someone to fill my shoes.' Kathy smiles knowingly. 'I heard your mum singing backstage. She's really good, isn't she?'

'Yes, she is.' I glare at Kathy. 'Did you "go missing" on purpose, Kathy?'

She looks at me, shocked. 'Me? Of course not. I'm just Kooky Kathy. I'm very unpredictable.'

'Well, are you going to be predictable for the rest of the show?'

She rubs Mr Piddles under the chin. 'Yes. Yes, I believe I will be. Mr Piddles will keep me in line. Won't you, little buddy?'

To be honest, I do trust that ferret more than I trust Kathy.

The crowd roars and Mum exits off stage as kids run on to perform 'Alarm Clock Assembly'.

'How was it?' she asks, panting and out of breath but alive with excitement. Her eyes sparkle in a way I don't think I've ever seen before.

'You were totally awesome, Mum!'

Mum looks up to see Kathy. 'Kathy! Am I glad to see you. That was amazing but I really don't need the pressure of a whole show.' She quickly takes off the coat and passes it to Kathy, who puts it on, then peels the stuffed ferret off and replaces it with the real thing. Mr Piddles rubs himself against the velcro, getting his scratch on. Mum clips the microphone onto Kathy's shirt collar and tucks the battery pack into the coat pocket.

'All right, let's do this!' Kathy announces, dramatically flicking her coat-tail behind her as she struts towards the audience.

'Kathy!' I yell. 'You're supposed to enter from the other side! And take the audience with you to your Lego house!'

'Yes, of course,' she says, turning on her heels and heading in the other direction. 'I knew that. Don't worry, it's all completely under control.' She strides off confidently in the other direction.

'Completely under control?' Mum asks.

I shrug. 'With Kathy, when is anything *completely* under control?'

The show goes past in a blur of running around, playing guitar, giving directions backstage, organising people, playing guitar again, helping Mrs Moshie find Stevie (he was hiding under Flynn's piano), moving the band from scene to scene (Detective McKenzie and his team have the audience completely under control), a bit more guitar and mostly dealing with all the nerves – a feeling very similar to that time I ate an entire showbag full of stuff when I was four, including a tub of glitter slime.

It's almost time for the big finale number. It will start with just Flynn and I on stage. Guitar and piano under a spotlight, all eyes on us. As my anxiety builds, I wish I could go back in time and rewrite the musical and give this number to someone else to perform. Someone like Kathy, who never seems to get nervous.

'You gherkin ready for your big whoop moment?' Flynn nudges me with his shoulder and gives me the number three. 'Whoops, I meant this.' A thumbs-up this time.

'If by ready, you mean ready to vomit all over my own guitar then yep, totally ready!' I say.

'Well, I can't gherkin wait to be on stage stop with my best mate. Rodgers and gherkin Hammerstein eat your stop heart out. Hammerstein's an upside-down gerbil!'

I laugh and the nerves melt a little.

'You gherkin got this!' Flynn says. 'If there's one gherkin thing you must have stop learnt by now wheeee, it's that you can do gherkin anything.'

'You know what?' I say, putting my guitar strap over my head. 'With you here, I reckon you might just be right.'

'That's the gherkin spirit. Now, let's – boil a football in salsa!'

I crack up again and the nerves melt a little more. 'We could do that, or . . .'

'Let's gherkin rock!'

We fist bump and walk out into the dark, taking our place on the front steps of Town Hall.

A spotlight comes up on Flynn and I. We're centre stage. Flynn's fingers glide across the keyboard and I softly strum the pick against the guitar strings.

Sometimes you think you're alone in
this life
That you're singing your very own song.
Until one day you sing just a little
bit louder
And now everyone's singing along.

Stop hiding yourself, head up, look around
You're surrounded by people who know
If they scratch at your surface, they'll
soon discover
The real 'you' that lies just below.

They make you laugh when you feel
kinda down
And will be there if jokes are
not working.
You finish each other's sentences too
That's not hard, if it's usually
'gherkin'.

Most importantly you know that you're
never alone
In a town that is chock full of friends.
We may draw the curtain on our
show tonight
But the story of Watterson never ends.

Now here we stand, a community
To conquer all that stands before.
Hand in hand, we form a family
With town spirit at its core.
I have your back and you have mine
On our shoulders, the short are tall.
Here we stand, stand for Watterson
And Watterson, we stand for all.

The lights drop and there's a moment of silence before a loud roar fills the air. For just a second I think a thunderstorm has hit and then I realise it's applause. Loud – very loud – applause for *our* musical. Flynn grabs my hand and drags me into line with the rest of the cast as the lights lift and we take a bow. I look out over the sea of people, thousands of hands clapping furiously. My arm is dragged down into a second bow and the roar lifts to another level. The applause swirls around us and I feel like it's almost lifting me off the ground.

We did it. Us. Me and Flynn. And Mr Deery, Kathy, SOBMA, Mum, all of Watterson. I have no idea if the huge crowd raised enough money to save the arts teachers' jobs, but when I look over at Ms Fox – standing in front of the band, taking her own bow – I think that maybe I did something even more important. Maybe I showed her that we care. Not just me and the rest of her music class, but all of Watterson.

Mr Deery walks out in front of the audience with a microphone and waves his arm towards us. 'One more round of applause for the creators of this amazing show, Mac Cooper and Flynn Vanderberg.'

'That's gherkin us,' says Flynn, and I feel a gentle shove on my back. We step forward and take a bow, and the roar swells up again. Now THIS I could get used to.

'Cooper and Vanderberg!' Mr Deery booms our names again.

Another roar, another bow.

'Now, maybe you two would like to say a few words?' Mr Deery says quietly, and passes the mic to Flynn.

'I'll gherkin keep this brief, because stop even my gherkin "brief" can be quite whoop long. I just want to gherkin say a huge – the marshmallows are on me. No they're not, you have to buy your gherkin own. A huge gherkin thank you to everyone who was a part of this wheeee production. And, of course, to my gherkin best friend – superglue the bananas together – my best friend gherkin, Mac. Who I will now hand the mic to whoop because he is way gherkin better with stop words than me. Wheeee!'

I take the mic. 'Not so sure about that, Flynn.' I look out into the enormous crowd. Mum and

Stevie and Mrs Moshie stand at the front. Mum's grinning at me like she's in a toothpaste commercial, Stevie's waving non-stop and Mrs Moshie is awake, which is something in itself.

'Um, hi, everyone. Thanks heaps for coming. Ah, so there was a particular reason we put on this show – not just that Flynn and I are obsessed with musicals and we thought it might earn us some brownie points with Mr D here,' I say, gesturing to Mr Deery. 'We wanted to raise some money for a cause that's really close to our hearts. Ms Fox, can you come up here?'

Ms Fox slowly steps up onto the stage. She's nervous and awkward, which is good, 'cos now I don't feel alone.

I take her hand and turn back to face the huge crowd.

'This is Ms Fox, everybody. She's my music teacher and she's the greatest teacher on the planet. Sorry, Mr D.'

Mr Deery smiles and shrugs. 'Can't win 'em all.'

'And she's not the greatest just 'cos she teaches us cool stuff, but because she lets us be us.

She doesn't expect everyone to be good at music, she just wants everyone to love it.'

Ms Fox squeezes my hand.

I hold her hand tight and continue. 'A couple of months ago I found out that Watterson Primary will have NO arts program next year. No art, no drama, no music. Which means no Mr Dinesh, no Mr Hubbard and no Ms Fox. And no place for kids like me to shine.'

Mr Deery ushers Mr Hubbard and Mr Dinesh on stage to join us. Tess Heckleston and Toby Baker carry a box on stage behind them.

'The whole reason we put this show on was to try to raise enough money to fund the Watterson Primary arts program for at least another year.'

I look down to Stevie waving at me. 'I really want my little brother to have a Ms Fox in his life.'

Tess and Toby push the box in front of the teachers.

'I don't think there's enough here, but we want you to have it anyway. Maybe you can teach one day a week or something? So the kids next year don't miss out completely?'

Ms Fox gives me a squeeze and takes the mic. 'I think if there's one thing tonight's performance has showed us, it's that our community needs an outlet for its artists. So while we think what you've done is wonderful, Mac and Flynn, Mr Dinesh, Mr Hubbard and I would love to donate these proceeds to fixing Balthazar Theatre so that everyone in our town has a place to enjoy shows like this. And maybe we could start some community art groups. What do you think, Mac?'

'Honestly?' I say. 'I feel like we always have to compromise. Watto Mall doesn't have to decide between a one fast food place or another. But it's your money – it should go where you want it to. Fixing up Balthazar Theatre is a pretty good use for it.'

Mr Deery leans into the mic. 'Jen, how about you get up here?'

Jennifer Heckleston walks through the crowd, which parts for her to pass. When she gets to the stage, she turns to me. 'Look, Mac, I know where you wanted this money to go. Are you sure?'

I nod. 'The theatre needs saving too.'

She smiles. 'Well, we do appreciate it. So much. I promise every cent will go into creating a space where more shows like this can happen.'

'Cool!' says Tess, cracking the lid of the box open.

Her mum snaps it shut. 'Don't even think about it!'

Flynn puts his arm around my shoulder. 'I guess we gherkin didn't quite get the stop ending we were gherkin after, did we? Whoop!'

'I wouldn't quite say that!' Mayor Wu pushes his way through the crowd and joins us in front of the audience. 'Can I borrow that please, Mac?' he asks, reaching for the microphone. I hand it over. I know opening night speeches are to be expected but this is getting a little ridiculous.

'Hi, everybody,' the mayor says. 'Firstly, I'd like to thank everyone for coming to this incredible show tonight. I think we can give one more round of applause to these amazing creators.'

The crowd roars again. I'll never get tired of that sound.

'For those of you from out of town, my name is Henry Wu and I'm the mayor of Watterson. The very proud mayor. But something was brought to my attention recently that *didn't* fill me with pride.

'An education without the arts is not an education. Without kids like Mac and Flynn being inspired at school, we risk a future with no movies to watch, no books to read, no art galleries to visit, no shows to see and no music to listen to. That sounds like a very bland future to me.'

Another round of applause from the audience. This time with a different energy – a sort of uprising.

'I've spoken to Mrs Keiren, and I know she is dealing with budget cuts but I just cannot support a school with no arts program. Not in my town. And as my daughter tells me, when the going gets tough, the tough get creative. So, a friend of mine and I put our heads together. Chad, do you want to come up here?'

'Who the gherkin is Chad? Stop,' asks Flynn.

'I have no idea,' I say.

'No way!' Tess whispers next to us.

I turn to her. 'What? Who is it?'

'The same person who always turns up at the end of these things,' Tess says. 'Someone is SO getting arrested.'

Senior Detective McKenzie joins the mayor on stage.

'Did we break some kind of law?' I ask Flynn.

'Lock the hippo in a jail! I don't gherkin think so.'

We both face Tess.

'Don't look at me!' she says. 'Why does everyone ALWAYS look at me!?!'

Mayor Wu continues. 'So Chad and I have been discussing the current situation. The money that young Tess Heckleston here found earlier this year was returned to the police department as evidence in the case against Scott Anderson. With his trial complete, and him now serving his sentence, that money was forfeited to the Minister for Finance.'

Mayor Wu hands the microphone to the detective.

'Yes, that's correct, Mr Wu. And as the community that the tainted funds originated from, Watterson can apply to have that money invested back into the precinct. Mayor Wu and I have been working hard to file an application to fund a special project to address education in the Watterson area. And as of this afternoon, the application was approved and the $900,000 will be returned to the town of Watterson.'

'WHAAAAAT!?!' I gasp.

'Buy a mansion with laser sharks!' says Flynn.

Mayor Wu grins at me. 'And that money is going straight back into Watterson Primary to refund the arts subjects and keep all of these wonderful teachers in their jobs for the foreseeable future!'

A huge roar from the crowd, a massive hug from Ms Fox, high fives all around, Mum blowing me kisses with pride in her eyes, and from Flynn . . .

'Mayor Wu is an astronaut monkey! You're not, Mayor gherkin – Mayor gherkin – Mayor Wu, you're gherkin awesome. Throw donuts at him!'

'Wait, wait, wait!' yells Tess. 'So let me get this right. The money *I* found is the same money that's going to save the school? So essentially I'm the hero here, right?'

Jennifer Heckleston glares at her daughter. 'Not now, Tess!'

Tess shrinks back. 'Okay, okay, I'm just saying. A hip-hip-hooray wouldn't go astray!'

'We gherkin did it!' Flynn says, grabbing me by the shoulders and shaking me. 'The perfect gherkin ending! We couldn't have stop written it any whoop better!'

I'm grinning so much I think I might have pulled a cheek muscle. Flynn's right, it's the perfect ending. All we need now is the encore!

ACT THREE

Scene Four

It's the end-of-year awards assembly at Watterson Primary. Everyone has showed up. Flynn and his parents even came and are sitting with Mum, Stevie and Mrs Moshie. Casey's dad and grandpa are in the front row along with Zeke's parents and Cookie's dad and his partner, Aaron. Kathy's here, joining the Hecklestons, and Toby Baker's mums sit behind them. I'm pretty sure I caught a glimpse of Mr Piddles, but if Mrs Keiren gets wind that there's a ferret in the hall, he'll be booted out the door. I think he's staying carefully hidden under Kathy's hair.

Ms Fox conducts the Year Five/Six band and choir as we perform. Sweat drips onto my guitar. It's sweltering. The school can only just fit in the hall normally, so with everyone's extended families showing up, people are jammed into every corner –

like when you try to push as many marshmallows as you can into your mouth.

Despite the heat, there's a cool vibe in the air. It's the end of school, so the kids are stoked. Us Year Sixers are moving on to high school. Parents are feeling proud.

In fact, the only person not smiling is Mrs Keiren. No surprises there. By the look on her face, she doesn't entirely approve of Ms Fox's song choice – 'Good Riddance' by *Green Day*. I know the song off by heart, so I can play along as I let my eyes and mind wander over the assembly.

I'm gonna miss this school. I never thought I'd say it, but I am. It feels like home. High school feels like a big, scary, foreign land that I'm not ready for. But I wonder if you're ever really ready for any change. It doesn't matter, I guess, 'cos it comes flying at you full speed and you just gotta choose whether you roll with it or fight against it.

My eyes fall on Flynn, who gives me a thumbs-up (and some rock hands and the rude finger for good measure). He waves his hands apologetically for that last one.

I smile. High school might be a bit scary, but I'll have Flynn. And nothing seems that scary with Flynn along for the ride.

We finish the song to a round of applause and one last disapproving glare from Mrs Keiren. As we step down from the stage and find our seats in the hall, Mrs Keiren approaches the lectern.

She taps on the microphone. 'Quiet down. Take your seats.'

The mumbling dies down and she waits until all you can hear is the sound of parents fanning themselves with the assembly programs and the occasional squawk from someone's baby sibling.

'Thank you, everyone, for coming today to celebrate the end of yet another school year. As well as an awards assembly, we are also here to announce our new Year Five leadership and, of course, it's graduation day for our Year Sixes, who are leaving us to face the challenges of high school. I am very happy to have seen you all grow and move on.'

'I *bet* she's happy to see you all move on!' Tess whispers behind me. 'She'll be even happier to see the back of ME the year after.'

Flynn and I snigger. I'm not sure that's what the principal meant but she certainly has a way with words.

'We now have a few awards to give out to our Year Fives and Sixes. These awards are voted by both peers and faculty. And whilst I do have a singular vote, I do not have final say or approval of the recipients. I just want to make that clear.'

Some whispers spread throughout the hall. I don't know what she means, but clearly ol' Principal Chicken is not happy with some of the winners.

'We would like to thank some special guests who have come to present the awards today. Please make them feel welcome, Watterson Primary.'

A round of applause fills the air as Senior Detective MacKenzie makes his way onto stage.

'Thank you, everyone, and thank you, Mrs Keiren. Despite our chequered past, it gives me great pleasure to present the award for Most Improved Young Watterson Citizen to someone who has grown a lot over this last year and proved that she can use her incredible strength of character, determination and entrepreneurialism for good. Please put your hands together for criminal-catching, fundraising and leadership extraordinaire, not to mention member of the SRC and next year's school captain, the one and only, most improved . . . Tess Heckleston.'

I spin around to look over my shoulder. Tess sits there in shock, her mouth wide open. Her mum, Jennifer, stares at her with a matching goldfish expression.

'Did they just say your name, Tess?' ask Jennifer.

'I highly doubt it,' says Tess.

'They did!' yells her dad. 'Go on, get up there!'

Tess stumbles out of her seat and up onto the stage. She accepts her award from the detective, who then directs her over to the principal. Mrs Keiren leans down and pins the school captain badge to Tess's t-shirt.

'I guess congratulations are in order?' says Mrs Keiren.

'It's okay,' says Tess sympathetically. 'I know this can't be easy for you.'

'And while we're at it,' continues Detective MacKenzie, 'let's bring up next year's vice captain – none other than . . . Toby Baker.'

'YAHOO! Whoop, whoop, whoop!' I'm pretty sure that came from Toby's mum, Fara.

Toby bounces up on stage and stands next to Tess. Mrs Keiren pins his badge on too. 'Keep an eye on her won't you, Mr Baker?' she says.

'Always!' grins Toby.

He grabs Tess's hand and raises it into the air as they pose for the bunch of phones pointing in their direction. Toby's mums and Tess's dad and sister are snapping away, but behind me I hear a little sniffle. I turn around to face Jennifer.

'You all right? I ask.

She nods and quickly rubs her nose. 'Just a bit proud, you know?'

I smile. 'You should be,' I say, and turn back to cheer them on.

Mrs Keiren returns to the microphone as Toby finally drags a STILL-bowing Tess off stage. 'To present our next award, we have a member of the Watterson Council. As Mayor Wu is here in his role as a father today,' Mrs Keiren gestures towards the mayor, who sits with his arm around Casey, 'we would like to welcome Deputy Mayor Claudio Lastra to present our next award.'

The deputy mayor steps up to the microphone.

'Thank you, Principal Keiren, and thank you for having me, Watterson Primary. Today I will be presenting the Earth Bound Award for greatest contribution to preserving our environment. It is my absolute pleasure to call up a group of young activists who changed many lives this year and changed our town for years to come. Please put your hands together for Casey Wu, Zeke McKillop and Chloe "Cookie" Munsta, or, as we all know them – the Green Peas.'

The school erupts as the original Green Peas make their way onto stage and collect their awards. Casey motions towards the microphone and Claudio steps aside.

Casey stands on her tippy-toes and pulls the microphone down. 'Thank you so much for this award and, while we really appreciate it, we also know it's important to acknowledge that Green

Peas is more than just us, and change is brought about by people getting together and demanding change. So it's only fair that ALL the Green Peas come up on stage for this one!'

'Get on up here!' yells Zeke.

Half the school jump out of their seats and head up on stage for a massive group bow. After a million photos, Casey makes her way back to her family and takes her seat.

'PPPPPPPFFFFFFTTTTTT!'

Casey glares at her grandpa as she reaches under her butt and pulls out a deflated fart cushion. 'Really, Ah Gong? A fart cushion? Aren't we a bit beyond that?'

Her grandpa is busting himself laughing. 'An oldie but a goodie, just like me!'

Mrs Keiren, having finally ushered everyone off stage, readjusts the microphone before introducing the next presenter. We cheer our way through a bunch of awards for academic achievements, artistic prowess and Anishka Batan even got a sport award despite almost taking Ms Mezher's head off with a soccer ball last month. If you ask me, it's actually Ms Mezher who's been the 'good sport' this year!

Mrs Keiren takes the microphone again. 'For our final award, we have a very distinguished guest. She's made a special trip to our little town to show her support for a young man with whom she shares a unique passion. Please put your hands together for Broadway musical sensation, and current star of *Matilda*, Kay Angelos.'

Flynn grabs my knee hard, making me jump in my seat.

'KAY ANGELOS IS A HIGHWIRE POLAR BEAR!'

Everyone turns to face Flynn as Kay Angelos makes her way on to the stage.

'I'm gherkin sorry. Whoop!' Flynn manages. 'But THE gherkin Kay Angelos is in whoop Watterson. Kay works in a fart cushion factory! Sorry, Kay. I know you gherkin don't.'

Kay grins as she approaches the microphone. 'Sometimes I wish I did. And I would certainly enjoy being a highwire polar bear, I'm sure.'

Flynn blushes, gives some rock hands and sinks into his seat a little. I whisper to Flynn,

'I can't believe Kay Angelos is here. Did your dad organise this?'

Flynn shakes his head. 'I don't gherkin think so.'

Part of me is sure this *can't* be possible – Kay Angelos at *our* school – but the other part of me knows there's probably not a lot of Kay Angelos impressionists floating around out there, and the person on stage looks *a lot* like her.

I can feel Flynn ticcing beside me, trying to keep his excitement under control instead of bursting out of him. But I get it. Kay Angelos is here. KAY ANGELOS! First she tweeted about our show, now she's turned up at our end of year assembly – what is going on?

'So, thanks for having me, Watterson Primary. When Mrs Keiren first told me about two kids writing an entire musical to raise money to save the school's arts program, I thought maybe she meant a little one-song show or something. But when she snuck into rehearsals to film bits and send them to me, I was absolutely blown away with what was being created.'

Wait a second! Mrs Keiren was the one who told Kay about our show?

Flynn stares at me. 'What the? Gherkin.'

I stare back. I didn't think Mrs Keiren even knew about our show, let alone cared. She'd been watching rehearsals? Wasn't she the one cancelling the arts program? Why would she care about saving it?

Kay continues. 'When Mrs Keiren taught me way back in the stone ages, she was always telling me off for singing non-stop and being such a show-off.'

Okay, now I can't cope – Mrs Keiren was Kay Angelos's teacher? I feel like I've slipped into some alternative universe.

'But since I started working in musical theatre, she hasn't missed a show. She says it's just because of the free tickets, but I know better.'

Kay looks to Mrs Keiren but her stone-cold face doesn't crack a smile. Kay laughs. 'She would never admit it, but she was very proud of all of you and what you were doing to save the arts in your school.'

I try to connect Kay's Mrs Keiren with the one I thought I knew. I remember what Mum said about her job at The Garage – 'Being near the top doesn't always give you the power to change things.' I always thought of Mrs Keiren as the boss, but maybe even she has someone above her. Somebody forcing change she doesn't want.

'And the least I could do is share the love. So thank you, Mrs Keiren, for sharing those videos with me and thank *you*, Watterson Primary, for showing how important the arts, and in particular musical theatre,' Kay winks at me, 'is to our community.'

Mrs Keiren is sitting dead still on stage. She looks so principal-y. But maybe underneath there's a real live human being? It's never occurred to me before, but maybe being a principal is not that easy a job. Maybe there's more to it than yelling into a loudspeaker and dealing with kids that are sent to your office for racing snails on the canteen tables.

Suddenly I feel real bad about all those times I joined in with the clucking as she walked by or agreed with kids when they blamed her for the play equipment being rusty.

'So without further ado,' Kay announces, 'please put your hands together for the recipient of this year's Arts Citizen award, Mac Cooper.'

Stevie squeals. Mum squeezes me in a bear hug and covers my squished-up face in a million mum-kisses. And Flynn yells . . .

'Mac for President of the banana tree!'

As I make my way out of the aisle, I grab Flynn's hand and drag him with me.

'Are you gherkin sure this is a stop good gherkin idea? Whoop!' he whispers to me.

'This would never have happened without you,' I say.

'But what if I gherkin say something stop embarrassing? In whoop front of Kay gherkin Angelos? Wheeee!'

I stop and turn to him. 'What if you do? You wanna miss the opportunity to meet Kay just because you might spit out a few gherkins?'

Flynn grins. 'No way!'

'Then move your butt!'

We leap onto stage to collect our award from Mrs Keiren. She raises an eyebrow as I drag Flynn up next to me. 'So this is the infamous Flynn Vanderberg?'

'Nice to whoop meet you Mrs Principal Chicken Keiren gherkin. Lay a dinosaur egg on stage. Bagaaaaark!'

I see Mrs Keiren's lips purse together and quickly jump in. 'Hey, thanks, Mrs Keiren. We wouldn't have had anywhere near as many people at the show if it wasn't for you getting Kay to tweet about it.'

'Yes, well, it's my job to support you all as best I can – whether I agree with your approach or not. Congratulations, Mr Cooper, award well-deserved.'

She shakes my hand firmly.

'You know what, Mrs Keiren, I think you might actually like us kids after all.'

Her eys narrow as she leans in closer and whispers to me. 'Please keep such opinions to yourself, young man. I have a reputation to maintain.' I zip my lips shut with a smile.

We head over to Kay and shake hands with her. Flynn's tics are ramping up as he stands next to Kay and the excitement on his face is impossible to hide.

I step up to the microphone. 'I just want to say, it might be me getting this award today but it's thanks to all of you. None of it would have been possible without your help. You're awesome, Watterson! Thanks.'

I move aside and open the mic for Flynn. He looks at me nervously.

'Go on,' I say.

Flynn steps up to the microphone, gives a thumbs-up and leans forward. 'Um, I just gherkin want to stop say one gherkin thing whoop . . . I . . . I love a hyena playing harmonica! GHERKIN!'

Stevie jumps up and yells, 'So do I!'

All the kids in the hall begin to cheer. 'Gherkin, gherkin, gherkin!'

I lean into Flynn. 'Is that what you wanted to say?'

'No, but I don't think I gherkin would have got this kind of stop response for saying, "Thank you, Watterson", so let's gherkin leave it on a whoop high!'

He grins at me and we walk off stage to chants of 'Gherkin, gherkin, gherkin!' around us. As we return to our seats in the audience, a bunch of kids get up and make their way back to the band area.

'Mac. Flynn.'

We look up to Mr Deery, who is now on stage with the arts teachers. 'I hope you don't mind, but a few of us got together to organise a little surprise for you.'

Mr Dinesh leans into the mic. 'A little "thank you", you might say.'

'Or a little "au revoir",' adds Mr Hubbard.

'Or maybe a little "you rock!"' says Ms Fox. She counts in the band and the whole school joins in to sing.

'Give It Up for Mac'

(to the tune of 'Stick It to the Man'
from *School of Rock*)

When the world is sucky
And wrong has come to town
Take a leaf from Mac's book
Don't take it lying down.

Our arts have now been saved
And no one got the sack
There's one kid to thank for it
Give it up for Mac!

It won't help to sit and pout
So get your mighty pencil out
They'll try and put you through your paces
But sing and dance right in their faces.
Learnt from the best, he ain't no hack
Give it up for Mac!

Who should get the credit?
Give it up for Mac!
Guitar, well he can shred it.
Give it up for Mac!
Got the coolest hair?
Give it up for Mac!
Who's our future mayor?
Give it up for Mac!

ACT THREE

Scene Five

The school holidays are almost over and I'll be starting high school soon. I'm not going to lie, I'm super nervous. But I'm not thinking about that tonight. Tonight is all about Mum.

After the musical, Mum started looking for a new job. With the live music being cancelled at The Garage so Bill could put pokies in, there was no reason for her to stay. But then, the day after our final assembly, the silent owner stepped in and cancelled Bill's lease. Next thing, Mum was acting like a super spy – having secret meetings, visiting the bank and BOOM! Before we knew it, Stevie and I were sitting at the kitchen table being told the Cooper family were the proud new managers of Watterson's innovative new art space.

I look around at the huge crowd who have turned out for the opening of The Wooden Fleet. Gone are the gross, sticky floors of

The Garage – when Mum took over, it got a complete renovation. The new venue is all wood, cosy tables and booths and, most importantly, a huge stage for live performances. Mum has worked out themes for each night of the week from All Out Rock, to Broadway Comes to Watterson, to Poetry Slam nights. She's really branched out to include her entire Watterson audience.

What Mum didn't tell us was that getting the lease meant our entire holidays would be spent cleaning and painting said new art space. But to be honest, it was pretty cool hanging out with Mum and Stevie and working on something together as a family. There's a little bit of each of us in here. Mum's signed Fleetwood Mac album hangs above the bar, Stevie's portrait of Tones and I decorates the door of the family-friendly room (we're saying it's an impressionist version because it looks a little more like a giraffe in a wig than the real thing) and right above the stage (yep, proud-mama placement) is a framed *Watterson: The Musical* poster. I've seen Mum Spray n' Wipe the glass at least ten times today. I keep telling her to give it a rest but secretly, I totally love it.

I walk back to our table from the bar and pass Flynn his lemonade. 'This gherkin place looks stop amazing, Mac.'

'I know. Mum really did an awesome job on it. I hope it's gonna work out for her.'

Flynn gives me rock hands and throws some lemonade at me at the same time. 'Sorry gherkin.'

I lick the lemonade off my hand. 'Drink it, wear it – all the same to me.'

Flynn grins and puts his drink on the table. 'I'm gherkin sure this place is gonna stop be a massive hit. Whoop! Don't headbutt the rock star!'

'Yeah, I think you're right. It's like Watterson has a new hunger for the arts. The place is already sold out for opening week and Mum has three exhibitions booked in. She's doing it all.'

'Did you gherkin find out who the stop secret gherkin owner is whoop?'

I look around the space as it fills with people, eying off each of them suspiciously. 'Apparently I'm gonna meet them tonight.'

I always thought Bill owned this place when it was The Garage, but turns out he was just renting. The person who actually owns the building wasn't too happy about Bill's pokies plan and decided it was time for a new tenant. I have no idea who it is but I can't wait to meet them and say thanks for choosing Mum.

I watch as Stevie drags Ms Fox by the hand around the place. 'And this is Mum's signed album,' Stevie explains. 'It's worth squillions of money.'

He absolutely loves Ms Fox already and he hasn't even started school yet. He came back from his orientation day and informed me that I was no longer Ms Fox's favourite and that he had taken my place. 'She's my teacher now, not yours,' he said, sticking his tongue out to emphasise the fact. I'm not gonna lie, I am just a *little* bit jealous. But I also couldn't be happier.

'Hey, kids!' Mum bounces over. She's beaming, with a smile that's been permanently plastered on her face. She looks like the entrance to Luna Park! Being Boss Mum really suits her.

'Hey, Mum.'

'Hi gherkin, Nikki.'

Mum puts her arms around both of us. 'Soooooo, how excited are we?'

'Tree frogs pee in a tornado!' Flynn laughs and shakes his head. 'Clearly very gherkin excited.'

I slide out of Mum's nervous squeeze. 'So when do I get to meet this silent partner of yours?'

She grins. 'Actually that's why I came over. They're waiting at the bar.' She takes both our hands and drags us through the crowd. 'Wait here,' she says, pushing us into the corner and running off.

'Do you gherkin reckon it's some big stop business tycoon whoop?' asks Flynn. 'Maybe I should have gherkin dressed up a bit. Wheeee!'

I shrug. 'It's probably someone from Claremont, or one of the people who owns those giant factories near the edge of town.'

'Hey there gherkin, buddy!' Flynn says. I turn over my shoulder to see Mr Piddles making his way along the bar. He runs straight past me, up Flynn's arm and onto his shoulders. Easy to see who's the favourite here. As always, Kathy is not far behind.

'Hello, kids!' she says, joining us at the bar. 'What's going down?'

'Going down?' I say.

'You know, what's up? What's happening? What're the headlines?' Kathy says, doing some weird thing with her hands that I think that *she* thinks is supposed to be cool.

I shake my head. 'Just waiting to meet Mum's secret business partner – the rich tycoon who owns this place.' I turn to Flynn. 'Maybe we should hide Mr Piddles in case they have an issue with ferrets in the building.' Flynn nods and opens the zip on his jacket. Mr Piddles ducks inside.

Kathy smiles. 'Anyone cool enough to own this place must be cool enough to love ferrets.'

I smile back at her, but I doubt it.

Mum comes rushing back. 'There you are!'

'I didn't move,' I say. 'So where's this high flyer?'

'Right here!' says Mum, putting her hand on Kathy's shoulder. 'Mac, meet our new business partner, Kathy.'

'Whaaaaaaat?'

'Put a werewolf in the shower!' says Flynn.

'But how? I . . . don't you . . .' Again, the words in my head refuse to exit my mouth.

Kathy shrugs. 'Turns out there are still a few buildings in Watterson that I own. Who would have thought? I mean, my parents used to own a whole bunch but after the will dispute and the court cases – well, I guess I sort of lost track. Turns out this little pad is still mine.'

'Wait,' I say, rubbing my forehead. 'You're trying to tell me you live in a Lego house in Brennan Park but you own an entire pub?'

'I know!' says Kathy. 'Go figure, right? It's been a while since I checked my records.'

I shake my head. 'There's no way. You can't not have known that.'

Kathy gives me a sideways smile. 'Who's to say what we know and what we choose to know. Or ignore. Or know we ignore.'

'Are you doing that Kathy-thing?' I say. 'Where you pretend you know less than you actually do?'

'I don't know what you're talking about.'

Flynn whispers to me. 'Is she making less gherkin sense than I do? Whoop!'

Kathy claps her hands together. 'Oh, and one more thing. Mac, will you do the honours?' She holds the big pocket of her jacket open.

I reach inside and pull out the little white ferret from Slater's.

Flynn freaks out. 'Lulu!' She leaps out of my hands and onto Flynn's arm, scurrying up to his shoulder and nestling into his neck like it's been her home for years.

'She's yours,' I say.

'To gherkin keep?'

'Yup, we already spoke to your parents.'

Mr Piddles ducks back to Kathy. She gives him a scratch behind the ears. 'Mr Piddles will be very happy to have someone to play with.'

'I gherkin love her!' Flynn says, rubbing his chin into her fur. 'Thanks, Mac. Whoop. Thanks, Kathy.'

'All right,' announces Kathy. 'Enough with the belated Christmas. Isn't this an opening night? Let's get this party started!'

With that, she leaps up onto stage and grabs the microphone. 'People, pets, patrons and polar bears, can I please have your attention!'

The crowd quietens down and turns to face Kathy.

'It is with great pleasure that I introduce our first performance of tonight – the grand opening of The Wooden Fleet, a creative space to welcome, display and celebrate the arts community and the creative force of Watterson. Without further ado, please put your hands together for Watterson's favourite duo – sporting a most excellent new title – Mac Cooper and Flynn Vanderberg of THE GHERKIN GUYS!'

The crowd roars as we take our place on stage. Flynn settles in at the piano and I stand at the microphone with my guitar.

'Thank you, everyone,' I say, my voice echoing around Mum's new space. 'This is a little song that Flynn and I wrote especially for tonight. We hope you enjoy it, and we hope you all have an awesome night here at The Wooden Fleet.'

'And we hope you all – dance like an octopus on a tricycle!'

I laugh. 'Yes, that too. And a five, six, seven, eight . . .'

THE END

DID YOU KNOW ...

Like Flynn explains to Mac, Tourette's syndrome is a condition of the nervous system and causes people to have tics. Tics can be twitches, movements, sounds, words or even full sentences. People who have Tourette's don't have control over these tics.

When writing this book, Nat worked closely with the awesome (and hilarious) Jess Thom, who is a writer, comedian, artist, disability rights campaigner and all-round total legend! Jess also has Tourette's and, rumour has it, she leads a secret double life as a superhero called Touretteshero, creating a space to celebrate and share the challenges, humour and creativity of Tourette's.

Nat enjoyed working with Jess sooooooooo much and doesn't know how to thank her except to put this book out in the world and hope that it's just one of many more kids' books with neurodiverse characters to come. Nat also hopes that one day soon she'll be able to head over to the UK, meet Jess in person and maybe even take her out for some tea and biscuits . . . and gherkins!

There's also a long overdue thanks owing to Chad, who has been a constant wealth of legal and criminal knowledge (and anecdotes) throughout the three Watterson books. Just like Senior Detective McKenzie, he has always been there exactly when he is needed as a source of information, inspiration, support and good old belly laughs.

And, of course, Nat has to thank her grandma, who took her to see her first ever musical. That experience will always remain in her heart, as will her Little Granny.

ABOUT NAT AMOORE

Nat hates writing her own bio so she asked some kids to do it for her instead . . .

'Nat is completely zany and wild, she's definitely an over-grown child. She used to be an acrobat, that's why they call her Flying Nat.'
Elliot, 10

'She's very silly, pulls funny faces and makes me laugh . . . and is sometimes a little OTT.'
Emma, 9

'Nat is kind and friendly and funny, but
sometimes she does get a bit excited.'
Rosie, 6

'Nat is funny, kind, crazy and creative.
She loves snot and dancing.'
Annie, 8

'Nat is funny and she shouldn't wear white clothes
because she will just get pasta sauce on them.'
Sam, 4

'Nat is hilarious. She's the person to talk to,
and to read, if you want to get in a good mood.
She can think up lots of good stories.'
Elodie, 10

'She is kind, she is silly, she is funny and she
makes me laugh. And she's the best.'
Evan, 7

'Nat's funny. Mic drop.'
Ben, 10

MEET THE KIDS OF WATTERSON PRIMARY

THE HILARIOUS STORY OF ONE BAG OF CASH, TWO BEST FRIENDS AND A WHOLE LOT OF TROUBLE.

THE OUTRAGEOUS STORY OF THREE BEST FRIENDS, ONE GREEDY MAYOR AND A WHOLE LOT OF PRANKING.

THE ROCKING STORY OF TWO NEW FRIENDS, ONE ARTS FIASCO AND A WHOLE LOT OF MUSIC.

Tonight, we're gonna kidnap our best friend.
And tomorrow? We run.

Sticks, Maki, Jed and Tommy live on the same street. But the adults around them are making decisions that could tear the four friends apart.

When they discover their favourite comic book series is being made into a blockbuster movie, they know what they have to do. Get to the audition. Get the parts. Stay together.

Nat Amoore joins forces with acclaimed graphic novelist Mike Barry to bring you a story of four kids – and four superheroes – who are taking their future into their own hands.